Debt Crises

The Cause of
Recessions and Depressions

Victor W. Hatch

Dedication

To the memory of my son,
To my daughters,
Family and friends,
And to people everywhere.
May you all do well.

Table of Contents

Table of Figures

Introduction

I grew up as a child during the "great depression" of the 1930s. We lived on farms in northwestern Oklahoma and southwestern Kansas. During some of those years it was a struggle to get by; particularly when there was a very dry year and the crops dried up.

As an adult I have also experienced the effect of recessions; being laid off from work and having to seek employment at a reduced pay scale. I've witnessed others being laid off from work due economic downturns.

There is a great waste during recessions and depressions; people are certainly capable of continuing to work and contribute to their own and others welfare. There is much potential work that could be continued and should be continued during these periods that is not being done. It should provoke us all to anger that recessions and depressions should break down our economic system—they are totally unnecessary!

Can we not continue to provide food clothing and shelter and meaningful work to those who would and could contribute? We need teachers, police and firemen. Are we incapable of providing for our own welfare; repairing and building the roads and infrastructure we need? What prevents us from these accomplishments? Only our ideas that we must continue the economic system of the past!

It seemed puzzling to me during the 1990s depression in the US that people were willing to work, yet there was unemployment. Companies would willingly hire people if they had sales. Yet sales had dropped as the ability of people to buy had been reduced due to unemployment.

This led me to investigate why depressions and recessions keep occurring. I like to understand how things work. Clearly it was not because workers were unwillingness to work or of

1

companies not wanting to produce goods. So what is the cause? These events, "panics"(1), depressions and recessions have been occurring for centuries.

The message I want to convey is that the method by which money in created and put into circulation causes recessions and depressions. There is no mysterious cause of economic cycles; rather there is a cause that can be understood. This flaw in the economic system has been the cause of economic problems, recessions, and depressions (panics in the past) for centuries. It creates more debt than money—until there is a breakdown; a depression or recession!

"Those who don't know history are destined to repeat it." Edmund Burke. However it is not sufficient to just know history; one must understand the underlying cause of events. Without this understanding one is doomed to a repetition of the same problem, and so we have the repetition of recessions and depressions.

Many economic texts have been written about economic cycles such as the Kondratieff cycle(2). None have a clear description of the cause of economic cycles. Various things have been assigned as the cause of panics, recessions and depressions. It might seem that they are just the after effects of booms. But why do booms and busts occur? (The actions during a boom do aggravate the situation and bring on a bust more quickly and severely.) Is it a result of human nature, or the movement of the stars or the moon? Is it just periodic changes in the mood of consumers? Certainly the mood of consumers and investors has an effect but that mood is likely influenced by the amount of debt that they have and are they easily making ends meet. Does the future for them look good or doubtful?

None of the above are the cause of recessions and depressions.

It is the purpose of this book to describe and detail the cause of economic cycles, to show that there is a cause of panics, recessions and depressions. The cause can be readily understood and demonstrated with a simple computer program.

Debt Crises

It is now time to emphasize the cause of these events called recessions and depressions. (In the 19th century they were often called panics.). It is desirable to understand the cause of these events; recessions and depressions. The present system of money creation has caused much human illness, poverty, crime, hunger, starvation, homelessness, unemployment and hopelessness; even contributing to social breakdown and war. This is and has been a problem worldwide, so this is not just a message for the people of the United States but for people worldwide.

By understanding the problem we can devise a better system. It seems that our politicians, bankers and economists have been so caught up in trying to handle the immediate problems that they have never stepped back and examined and analyzed the present system. Had they done this it seems that they also would have come to the conclusion that the inevitable result would be a "great recession" or "great depression" or "debt crisis" periodically!

There is a better way of creating money and getting it into circulation. It should be done peacefully and not by revolution. If nothing is done the result will be continued cycles of depressions, recessions and excessive inflation. Economic problems in the past have contributed to revolutions and wars! We can and must change this system!

The preamble to the US Constitution states that the purpose of the Constitution is to "promote the general welfare". The present economic system fails in this regard.

This is a time of great problems like the debt crisis; it can be changed to a time of great solutions. Perhaps by great or just many projects—restoring infrastructure, getting water to deserts; all funded by the creation of debt free money! Let us create a turning point of renewal!

Chapter I: A History of Depressions.

Chapter II: The Effects of Depressions and Recessions.

Introduction

Does this country not have the resources to provide for most of the food, shelter, water, power systems, schools, roads and etc to provide a decent living for all of our people? And at the same time provide meaningful employment to workers to contribute to the welfare of themselves and others? Of course it does! Is this not true of many countries? The economic system is sadly awry!

Chapter I
A History of Depressions

Booms, recessions, depressions and panics have occurred repetitively over centuries, affecting the lives of millions of people. It should be kept in mind that each of the "panics", recessions and depressions have resulted in much human suffering, sickness and starvation, even contributing to wars.

Panics, recessions and depressions have occurred repetitively in the US in since the birth of the nation many prior to the "great depression" of the 1930s. Panics and depressions have occurred for centuries before the establishment of the United States of America.

Various causes are attributed to the panics and depressions of the 19th century. During each one of them there is the common theme of panics and bank failures. The panics were caused by banks not having enough money on hand to reimburse their depositors. The failure of one bank would often lead to a panic rush by depositors of other banks to withdraw funds. Thus a panic would spread and often lead to the failure of many banks. Companies and people would lose money on deposit with the bank spreading the economic downturn.

A panic occurred in 1819, then again in 1832, and 1836.

The panic of 1837 has been attributed to a real estate bubble. The money supply was greatly expanded when the Bank of The United States lost its charter (Vetoed by President Jackson.) and "free banking" followed. The banknotes of the various banks lost most of their value in the collapse. A six year depression followed.

The gold rush of 1849, resulted in money (gold) being dug out of the ground and put into circulation–thus avoiding a recession or depression for a number of years.

A History of Depressions

Twenty years after the "panic of 1837", was the panic of 1857. Next was the panic and depression of 1869 to 1871; then again a panic in 1873.

During these panics the loss of jobs and income by workers who were laid off from their jobs resulted in reduced demand for construction of factories and homes; demand for food, clothing, housing, horses, carriages, wagons and etc. (Many people were unable to buy food and clothing or pay rent.) This resulted in further deflation, i.e. prices falling.

The depression of 1893 was a very severe one which lasted into 1898. This depression started in Europe with bank failures, and spread to the United States. It was comparable in severity to the depression of the 1930s. Railroads, banks and many businesses failed. Unemployment was very high around 18% and higher in some cities. Many people were homeless and drifted about the country in search of work, food and shelter!

Gold from the Klondike, (Alaska) and Cripple Creek (Colorado) gold rushes helped pull the country out of this depression of the 1890s, by money (gold) being dug out of the ground and put into circulation! Gold from Australia and South Africa helped boost the world economy out of this depression.

A banking panic occurred in 1907. The value of stocks on the New York stock exchange fell. It was started by the failure of a bank and trust company, which spread to other banks. J.P. Morgan acted to stop this panic from spreading to the point of taking down most of the large banks by supporting them with funds and arm twisting other bankers to work together to stop the spread of this panic. Most notable about this panic is that it led to establishment of the Federal Reserve System in 1913 as a solution to the problem of bank failures, and to the concern of the power of J.P Morgan and "The Money Trust".

Following World War I there was the brief depression of 1920-1921. This was started by the Federal Reserve raising the interest rates to the suppress inflation that occurred after the end of World War I. This depression of 1920 created hardship for farmers and businesses. In the mid 1920s there was a real estate boom and bust; particularly in Florida.

In the late 1920s extending into 1929 there was a stock market bubble. Many investors who bought stock on margin (3), paying interest rates of 10 to 15 percent wound up losing; often not just money but also homes and business. Banks and insurance companies in addition to individuals were speculating on the stock market during this bubble. This bubble burst in 1929 resulting in the start of the "Great Depression" of the 1930s.

There were bank panics at this time which caused many banks failures with consequent loss by many depositors and investors.

The onset of this "Great depression" started in Europe and then in the US in 1929 and affected countries worldwide, in both Europe and Asia.

In the US the economy had started picking until 1937, and then in 1937 the Federal Reserve raised reserve requirements of member banks which then created a new downturn.

From "A Primer on Money"(4) "---*the Federal Reserve took certain deliberate actions to counteract or offset other events of the day. The best illustration of this involves a legislative action with which the writer* (Representative Wright Patman) *was personally concerned. It has to do with the so-called soldiers' bonus. Let me explain.*

During World I there was a great increase in wages and, of course, many "war millionaires" were made. Those who served in the Armed Forces, however, continued to receive a low rate of pay, appropriate to, if anything, the 1915 wage scale. Specifically, soldiers in France were paid $1 per day.

A History of Depressions

---*following the war Congress decided to adjust the pay of the World War I veterans retroactively. Instead of giving the soldiers their overdue pay in cash, however the Congress provided for it in what was called a delayed compensation certificate. These certificates were to be paid off in cash when the veterans reached a certain age.*

Now during the great depression, many of these same veterans were, of course, standing in breadlines, selling apples on street corners, and otherwise suffering in the fate of others in the great army of the unemployed. It occurred to me (Wright Patman) that under these circumstances, the compensation certificates should be paid in cash, without delay, not at whatever time the veterans reached the age specified in the certificates. Further it seemed to me that the release of such a large amount of cash by the Government would be beneficial, providing (or releasing) added purchasing power over the whole economy and thus helping to bring about economic recovery.

----*this proposal was finally successfully enacted in 1936. The delayed compensation certificates were paid in August of 1936, putting several billion dollars' worth of purchasing power into the cities, towns, villages, and farms of the country.*

-----*I was for several years puzzled as to why the release of these several billion dollars of purchasing power did not cause any big splash in the economic pond as I had expected, but indeed seemed to have no effect on the economy. In time I learned that in June of 1936, the Federal Reserve raised the reserve requirement of the member banks, in anticipation of the "inflationary" effects of the soldiers' bonus and, in fact, reduced the money supply of the country by almost the exact amount of the payments which the veterans received. The Federal Reserve prevented "inflation" to its way of thinking, but it proceeded to hobble the economy which had 17 percent of its workers already unemployed—and subsequently plunged the economy into the deadening relapse of 1937-1938."*

Debt Crises

World War II brought the country out of the "great depression" of the 1930s by government spending for armaments.

After the establishment of the Federal Reserve Bank in 1913; with the exception possibly for the recession of 1929 and the recession of 1974, the recessions in the 20th century correlate directly to the action of the Federal Reserve Bank in fighting "inflation". This was done by either the raising of interest rates by the Federal Reserve Bank or by increasing the reserve requirements of banks to fight "inflation". (As noted before; the Federal Reserve raised the reserve requirement of banks in 1936 which aggravated and prolonged the "Great Depression.)

In 1973 OAPEC (Organization of Arab Petroleum Oil Exporting Countries) plus a few other countries placed an embargo on oil, restricting the oil available to the western industrial nations, producing the 1973 "oil crisis". This plus a stock market crash may have been the primary cause of the 1974 recession.

A comparison of the events of the 1920s and 1930s with the events of the 1980s thru the first decade of the 21st century shows a number of similar events, a very similar pattern.

This depression of 1920-1921 was caused by the Federal Reserve raising the interest rates to suppress inflation that occurred after the end of World War I. Similarly starting in the mid 1970's interest rates were pushed up in the recession of 1974. Again the interest rates were raised in the 1980s, to fight inflation, peaking at over 20 percent and starting a recession. This was done as in 1920 to combat inflation.

The depression of 1920 and that particularly in 1980 created hardship for farmers and businesses; being unable to get loans for seed (the farmers) and increasing the cost of operation for both farmers and businesses. In 1980 many farmers were denied loans to continue operations—many farms were foreclosed; also many small businesses were forced to close their doors.

The high interest rates of the 1980s increased the value of the US dollar in relation to that of other countries. This made exports from this country overly expensive causing a continuing negative balance of trade for this country. This contributed to the loss of many jobs.

Commercial banks were speculating on the stock market in both the 1920s and in the later part of the 20th century. In 1933 the Glass-Steagall Act separated commercial banking from investment banking and forbid commercial banks from speculating. (Commercial banks were those banks that accepted deposits whereas investment banks were those that engaged in investments, such as financing businesses, helping businesses raising money such as by issuing stock.) This separation was done so that the Federal Deposit Insurance Corporation would not be supporting banks which engaged in investments and speculation. This restriction on banks was removed in 1999, by the repeal of the Glass-Steagall Act, by the Gramm-Leach-Bliley Act.

The Gramm-Leach-Bliley Act of 1999 and the prior deregulations of the 1980s and 1990s led to the "too big to fail" banks and insurance companies. This led to the banks and insurance companies being bailed out by the Federal Government. This was predicted by Representative John Dingell of Michigan during the hearing on the Gramm-Leach-Bliley Act in 1999.

In the 1920s and in the 2000s banks and insurance companies were speculating and financing speculation, in the late 1920s in the stock market, in the 2000s mostly in housing. In 1929 the stock market bubble burst; in 2007 the housing bubble burst. (The speculation in housing was a worldwide boom and bust—not just the US. So again we have a worldwide "recession".)

Debt Crises

There is a definite correlation between the high interest rates imposed by the Federal Reserve Bank and the recessions of the last 100 years "to fight inflation". Inflation cuts into banks profits by reducing the value of the money used to repay loans. However banks create inflation by increasing the supply of money. Bankers prefer high interest rates, low inflation and thus higher profits. It seems any justification would do to raise interest rates.

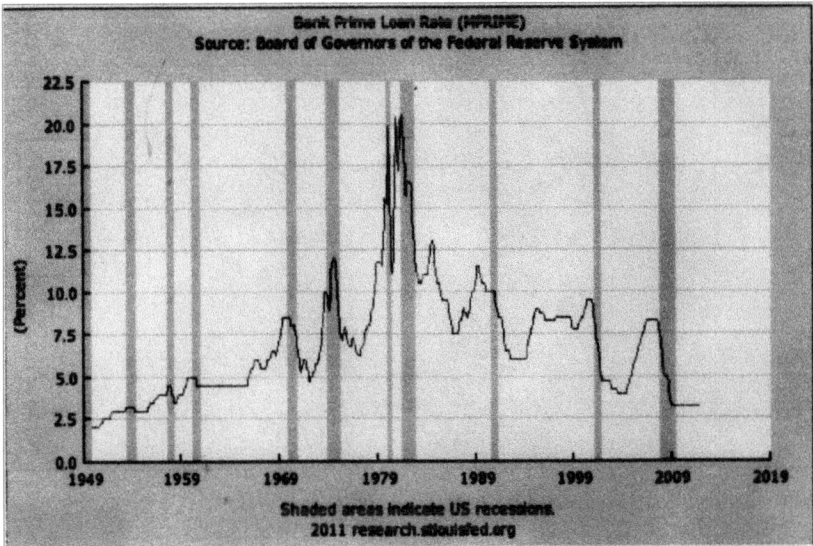

Figure 1. Prime loan rate. 1950—2010. From Federal Reserve Bank St. Louis.

The recessions of the late 20th century correlate with the raising of interest rates by the Federal Reserve, as shown in figure 1. The act of raising the interest rate was the jolt that started the recession at that time. The underlying cause was and is the excessive debt created by the method of creation of money.

This has been a brief description of the panics, recessions and depressions of the last two hundred years. Note that with

11

the introduction of Federal Deposit insurance there have been no more panics where depositors rush to get their money out of the bank before the bank closes its doors.

Chapter II
The Effects of Depressions and Recessions

Panics, depressions and recessions have been with us for many years and not just in the United States. They have occurred in many nations

Panics and depressions have occurred repetitively in the US prior to 1930.

These events, panics, recessions and depressions have resulted in poverty for many people and for wage workers often resulted in the overall average level of wages being near the starvation point. Many people then, out of necessity, rely on others; relatives, charity, food stamps and unemployment compensation to survive. This is sometimes bare survival. Poverty also makes people much more susceptible to illness and death. The suicide rate also increases during panics, recessions and depressions.

In the years and centuries prior to the depression of the 1930s not only was there no social security and unemployment compensation but instead there were debtors' prisons, poor farms and poor houses. Poor farms and poorhouses were established in the US in the early 1800s and continued through the 1930s.

The poor at times were considered unworthy or lazy or unwilling to work and therefore were not worthy of help. In some earlier times beggars were beaten severely to drive them out of a town or village.

Laws were and are even now on the books in some of the states of the US for a person to be imprisoned for debt.

When a bank failed due to a panic this often meant the failure of companies that had their funds on deposit with the bank. The failure of the bank would mean that the company could not obtain the funds that it had on deposit with the bank and could not pay their employees and suppliers. It also meant the individuals that had money on deposit with the bank lost their money; unless they were one of those that rushed to the bank soon enough to get their money before the bank closed its doors. There would thus be a downward spiral as the failure of a company would spread unemployment and further business failures.

This factor of the banks not having the funds to reimburse depositors was typical during panics and depressions prior to the creation of the FDIC (Federal Deposit Insurance Corporation) in 1933. Many banks failed in panics, depressions and recessions.

Before and during part of the "great depression of 1930" there was no Social Security, unemployment benefits, or food stamps. Consequently these panics and depressions resulted in many people becoming homeless; some turned into beggars and thieves. Near starvation made them more susceptible to disease, and meant starvation for some

The industrial revolution contributed to a great shift of population from the farms to the cities in the 19th and 20th centuries to work in the factories. The development of farm machinery added to this by reducing the labor needed for farming. The lack of support for the unemployed and homeless in the cities added to the misery and desperation of people during panics and depressions during the 19th and early 20th century.

At the start of the depression of the 1930s there was no FDIC (Federal Deposit Insurance Corp), so with the failure of banks many people lost their savings. There was high unemployment, factories shut down and etc. It certainly was not due to the unwillingness of workers to work, or of manufacturers to produce needed goods or farmers unwilling to grow crops and animals.

In the 1930s the unemployment rate was around 25% of the work force. In some cities it was higher. Many people were forced out of their homes. There were shanty towns around many of the cities; these were called "Hooverville's" after President Hoover, the president of the US during the early part of the depression. It was felt that Hoover was uncaring about the people since he took no action; except to have troops fire on WWI veterans who came to Washington to plead for the War bonuses they had been promised.

The unemployed, around 20% to 25% of the workforce, did not have the means to buy goods or food, thus the market for goods, services and food was considerably reduced. This contributed to a contraction of spending which then contributed to the further downward spiral of economic activity. Families became homeless; many farmers lost their farms. Some charities and churches set up soup kitchens. These however were inadequate to provide for the great need. Men rode the rails and begged for meals, perhaps doing some chores in exchange for a meal. Many people were turned into beggars and/or thieves.

During this depression there were many men out of work drifting about the country. Also many families left their homes in Oklahoma, Arkansas, Texas and Kansas, the "dustbowl" during some of the Depression years. Many migrated to California, some to Oregon.

This country did not completely recover from the 1930s depression until the government greatly expanded the spending for arms for WWII. Some countries which were devastated by the depression and then the war did not recover for a number of years after WWII.

There are a number of effects on people and society during a recession or depression. These effects include an increase in the death rate from heart disease and other illnesses. The effects also include an increase in suicides, admissions to mental hospitals, an increase in drug use and an increase in crime.

There is a great economic waste in unused human potential work during these periods!

There was no unemployment insurance, Medicare, food stamps or welfare programs at that time so the loss of a job often meant the loss of housing, and no means to buy food. Near starvation made them more susceptible to disease, and meant starvation for some.

The effect of this depression, the "great depression" of the 1930s, was made worse because it coincided with the dust bowl years; years of drought across the prairies of the western United States and Canada.

Possibly the worst effect which led to many of the others was the feeling of helplessness and hopelessness on the part of people to provide for themselves and their families.

This depression was not confined to the United States; it was a worldwide depression, starting about a year earlier in Germany. The failure of a major bank in Austria in 1931 spread panic through Austria and Germany. The high unemployment, poverty and inflation in Germany during the depression contributed to the rise of Adolph Hitler in 1933.

Hitler took advantage of the poverty during the depression to overthrow the government, which government was ineffective in counteracting the effects of the depression and the high inflation at that time. Similarly in Spain the consequent poverty and unemployment during the depression led to the Spanish civil war which started in 1936 and continued until 1939.

Japan experienced a financial crisis in 1927. During the "great depression" of the 1930s Japan experienced poverty, starvation and a famine. This contributed to the rise of the military in Japan, with the assassination of some politicians. So again we have depression contributing to war.

So the "great depression" of the 1930's was a great worldwide catastrophe; one might even say part of a world shaking catastrophe that included World War II.

The recession of 1974, which was due to the "oil" shock; shortage of oil and consequent high prices of gasoline and other fuels due the embargo placed on oil imports by AOEPC (Arab Oil Exporting Countries) at this time. This resulted in high unemployment and the consequent increase in sickness, suicides, homicides, more crime with the prison population increasing, more homeless people, increased admissions to mental hospitals, and more hopelessness with more drug addiction.

The recessions of the 1980's, which were started by the Federal Reserve Bank raising the interest rates extremely high, was even worse than that of 1974. There were many business failures, even large companies, many farmers lost their farms. Many workers were forced to accept lower pay. There were many suicides and families broken up.

The Federal Reserve raised interest rates very high in the 1980s, over 20% for a while, in the name of fighting inflation. Yet this inflation was caused by the increase in money supply created by the banks. The Federal Reserve could have acted to restrain the money supply by other means, such as placing restrictions on loaning money by the banks, or increasing the reserve requirements of the banks.

The recessions of the 1980s had another very serious effect. The high interest rates raised the value of the dollar in relation to the currencies of other countries. This made US exports more costly for other countries to buy and made imports much cheaper. This killed many businesses that were exporting products or competing with imports, with the consequent loss of jobs in these industries. At the same time the high cost of borrowing put many farmers, and companies out of business. So Americans were made poorer due to the cost of borrowing, and the loss of jobs due to high interest rates and the loss of jobs due to the negative effect on trade.

The present "Great Recession" (Which started in 2008 and is also a worldwide calamity for many people.) is far worse than the deep recession of 1974-75, so is the poverty; so must also be the human suffering, the loss of life and sickness! Many would be workers have given up trying to find jobs. The added factor of "free trade" has sent jobs overseas and sent trillions of our dollars overseas in the last three decades. (See "The Pooring of America"(5), which points out that Americans have been made poorer year after year since the advent of "free trade" starting in the 1970s.) This trade imbalance was aggravated by the effect of the high interest rates imposed. This was not a problem during the years leading to the depression of the 1930s, or during the 1974-1975 depression. This problem began in the 1980s with the raising of interest rates very high!

There is another effect of panics, recessions and depressions that contributes to the human poverty. From "A Primer on Money"(4) ,by Representative Wright Patman. *"Like powerful bankers who came after them, some of the goldsmith bankers were not free of suspicion that they deliberately precipitated depressions at times. At such times, when business firms were forced into bankruptcy, valuable assets could be bought up at bargain prices by those who possessed sufficient money—or could create it for themselves."*

In the present "great recession" we have had banking and insurance firms taking over other firms, also the taking of property by foreclosure for a fraction of its value. In the 1930s banks in farming communities took over farms which in later years they would then rent back to farmers.

Prior to the advent of deposit insurance, just the hint that a bank might fail could start a run (All the depositor rushing to get their money before the bank closed down.) on a bank causing it to fail; this could then lead to similar runs on other banks. This then would be the start of a "panic".

So for many people, in the low income and "middle class" recessions, depressions and "panics" are a disaster. There was during and prior to, many of the recessions, depressions and panics, a disproportionate shift of wealth away from the general populace to a small proportion of people. Many of us have experienced the negative effects of recessions as in being laid off from a job; having difficulties finding jobs, having family members in financial difficulty and etc.

The state laws against usury (limiting the interest rates that could be charged by banks) were removed by federal laws as a way for the Federal Reserve to fight the inflation of the 1970s' and 1980s'. This has allowed interest rates on loans and credit cards to be increased, at times near 30%. This has resulted in the interest rates for consumers rising very high for some, usually those least able to pay and causing more hardship. The least able to pay are charged with the higher interest rates because they are at higher risk of not repaying. Yet the higher interest rates make it more difficult for them to pay and contributes to poverty.

These high interest rates also reduced the purchasing power of individuals and companies, thus having a negative effect on the economy.

The most devastating effect is the loss of hope of people due to lack of useful work and inability to support or contribute to his family; being overly dependent on others. So we have the increase in crime, disease, suicides and etc. This has led to riots, revolutions and warfare with the death of many people and much destruction.

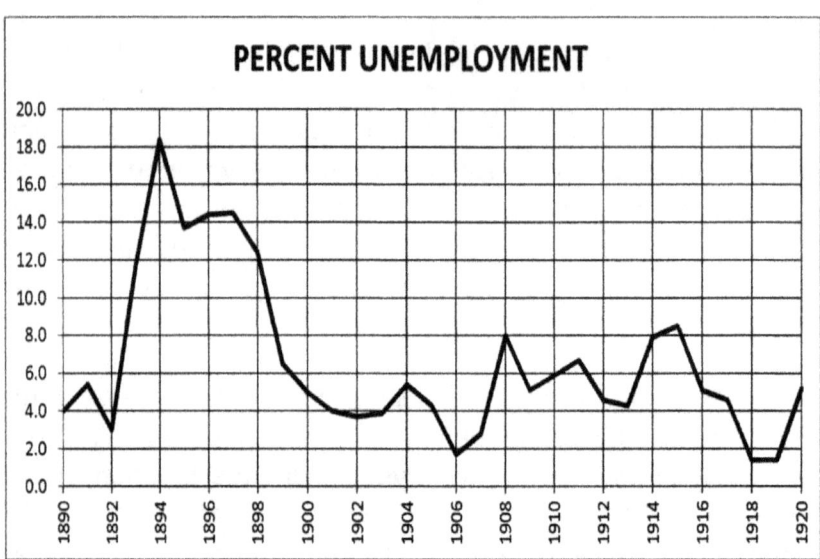

Figure 2. Percent Unemployment 1890—1920. Data from Census Bureau archives.

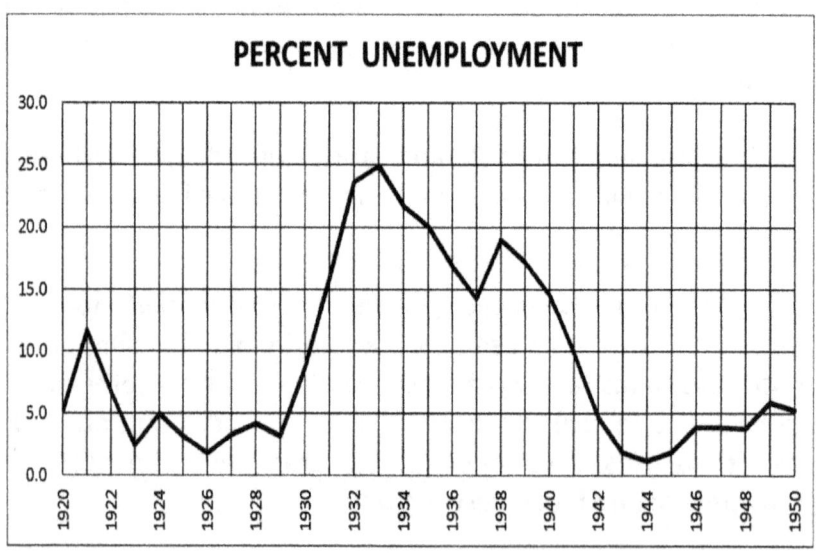

Figure 3. Percent Unemployment 1920—1950. Data from Census Bureau archives.

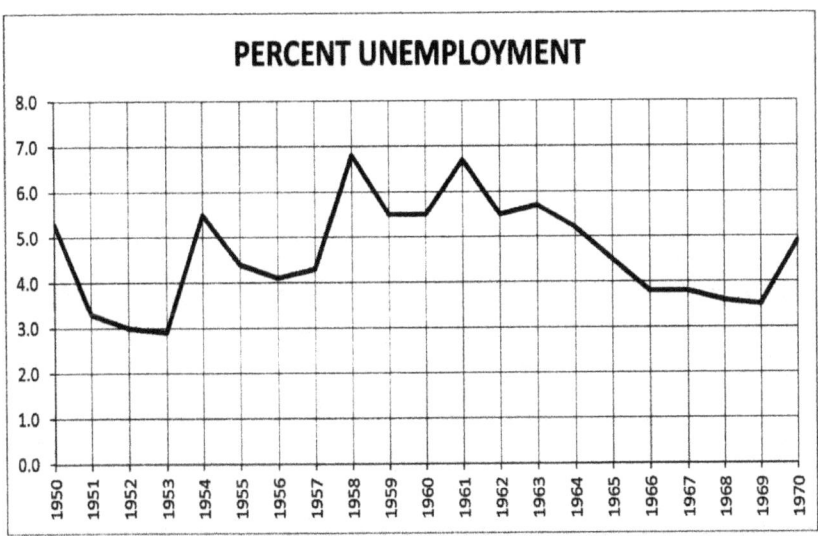

Figure 4. Percent Unemployment 1950—1970. Data from Census Bureau archives.

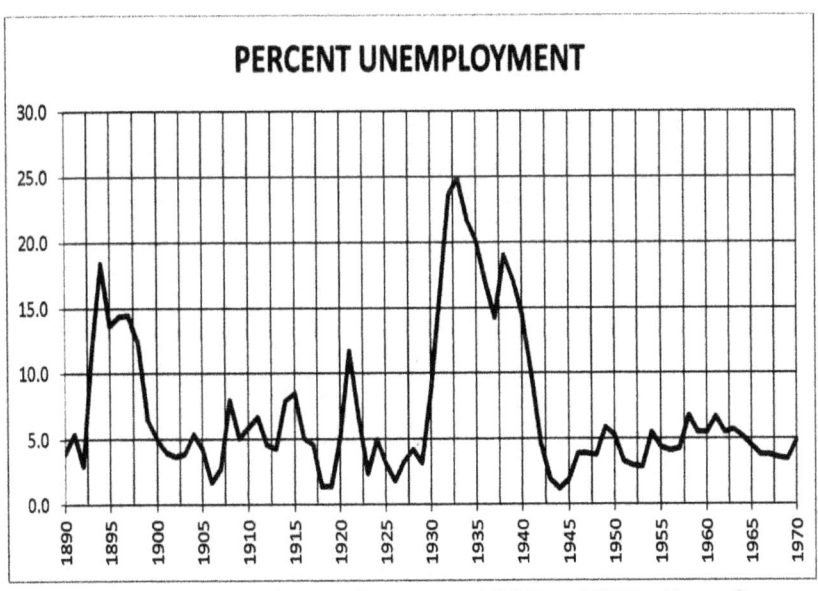

Figure 5. Percent Unemployment 1890—1970. Data from Census Bureau archives.

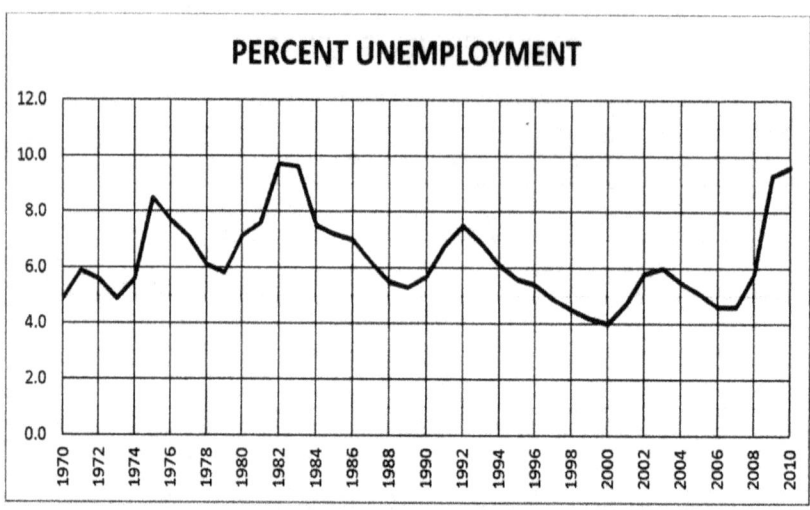

Figure 6. Percent Unemployment 1970—2010. Data from US Bureau of Labor Statistics

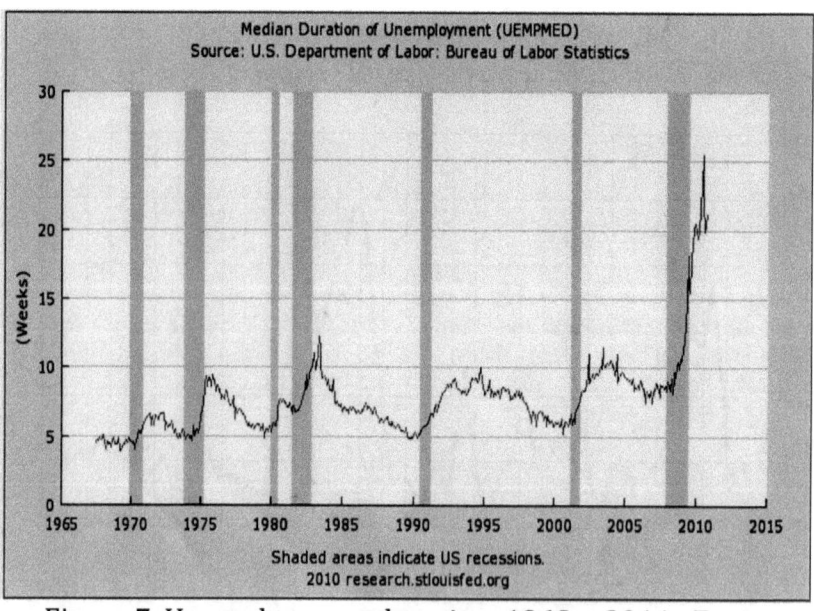

Figure 7. Unemployment duration. 1968—2011. From Federal Reserve, St. Louis.

Chapter III
Recessions and Money

Ever wonder why recessions and depressions keep happening? Recessions or depressions seem to keep occurring. They do not occur at regular intervals, but seem to occur at random intervals.

Herein it will be shown that recessions and depression correlate with a decrease in the rate of increase in the money supply.

About 1990 it struck me as strange that we were experiencing a recession. Workers were laid off from their jobs. Consumers had reduced their buying; this led companies to reduce their workforce. This reduction in the work force then led to a further reduction in sales; to a further reduction in workers; then a further reduction in sales—further reduction in sales—a downward spiral. This is the typical downward spiral of recessions and depressions!

As we have seen in the chapter about the history of panics, depressions and recessions, this collapse of our economic system has been repeating for centuries. The pattern is much the same each time, with much worse effects before unemployment compensation, Social Security, and deposit insurance for our bank accounts.

Why does this occur? It is not because of unwillingness of workers to work and hold a job. Most who are unemployed during a recession would gladly work if they were offered a job. If they had more sales companies would hire more workers.

The common factor then appears to be a lack of money in circulation; at the least not enough money coming into the hands of consumers. How does money come into circulation? Money might be likened to the medium of circulation of our economy.   As it circulates it provides the flow of energy throughout the economy. So the reduction of the flow of money reduces the economic activity.

It is not the inability of our people to work and produce the food, homes, autos, roads, electricity and other items needed by the people of this country. It is the breakdown of this circulation of money—the flow of the energy of the economy that creates recessions and depressions.

The volume of money supply designated M2 was 1.28 billion dollars in 1867; in 2010 M2 was 8.8 trillion dollars. M1 is the money supply that is readily available for spending: currency plus coin plus deposits in banking accounts, etc. M2 is M1 plus savings and time deposits that are not so readily available for spending.

Since lack of money in circulation during a recession or depression seems to be a common denominator of recessions and depressions does a look at the money supply confirm this?

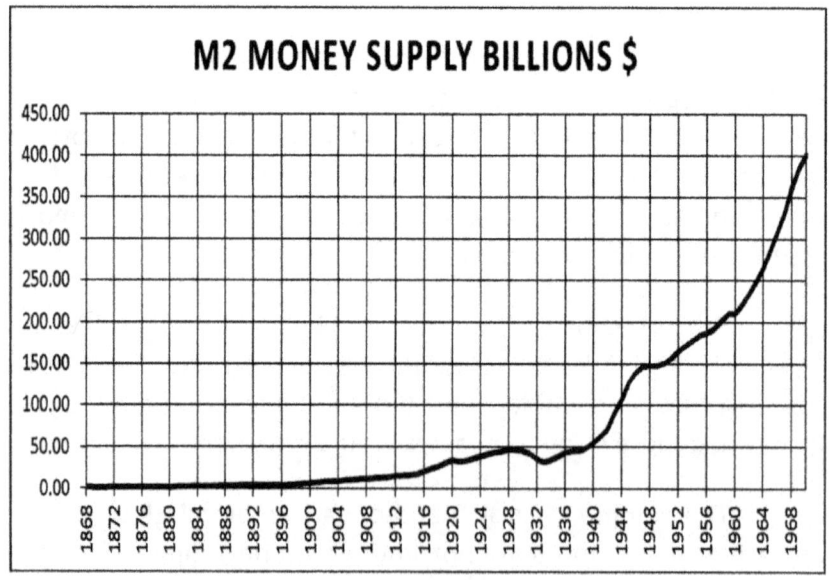

Figure 8. M2 Money Supply 1868 to 1970.

Figure 8 shows a continual increase of the money supply over 102 years. There is a downward spike during the 1930s. An increase in money supply is necessary with the increase in economic activity over time. Also an increase in money supply is necessary with the increase of the population.

A look at the rate of change of the money supply gives a better picture.

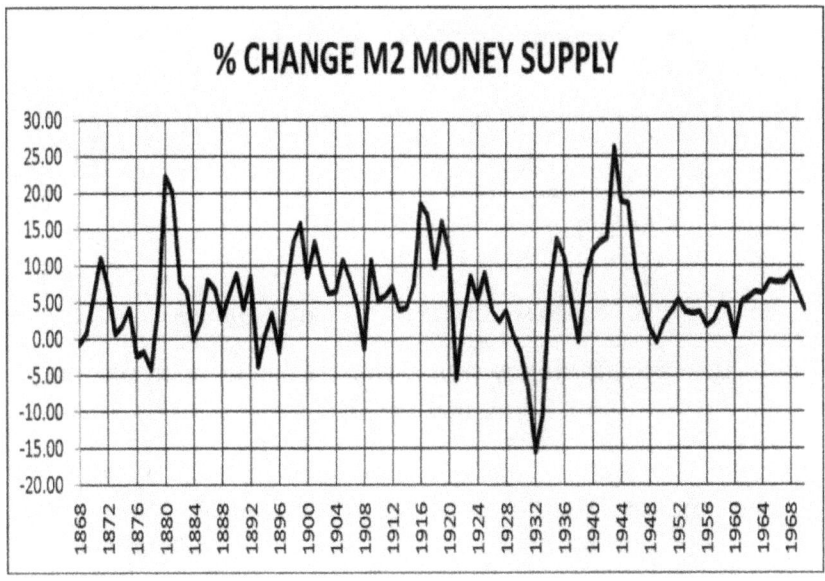

Figure 9. Annual percent change in M2. 1868—1970.

Here we see in figure 9 that the dips in the chart correspond to panics and depressions. A more detailed breakdown illustrates this better; particularly when unemployment is added to the chart.

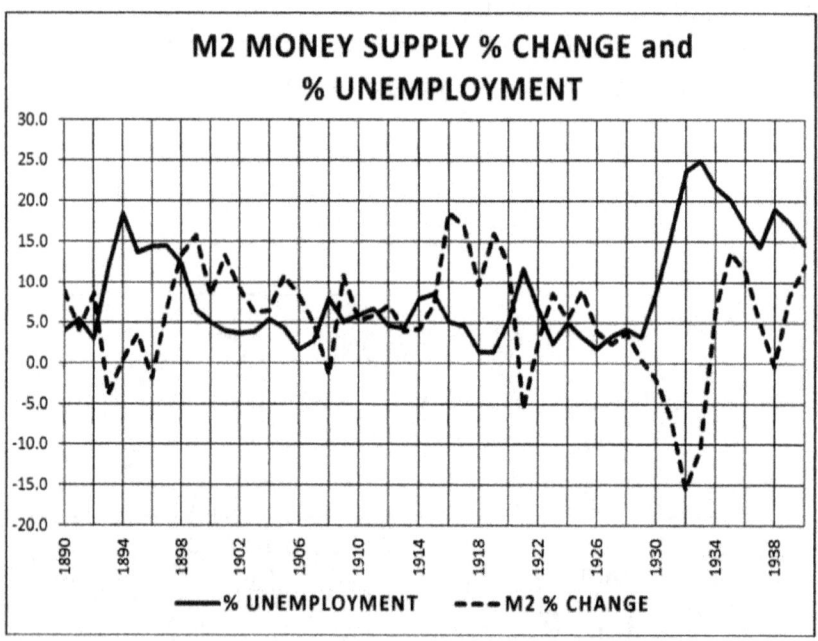

Figure 10. Percent money supply change versus unemployment. 1890—1940.

In figure 10 it is easy to spot the effect of the reduction of the money supply causing depressions. The severe depressions of the 1890s and the 1930s are easily seen. The change in the money supply change correlates inversely to the unemployment rate.

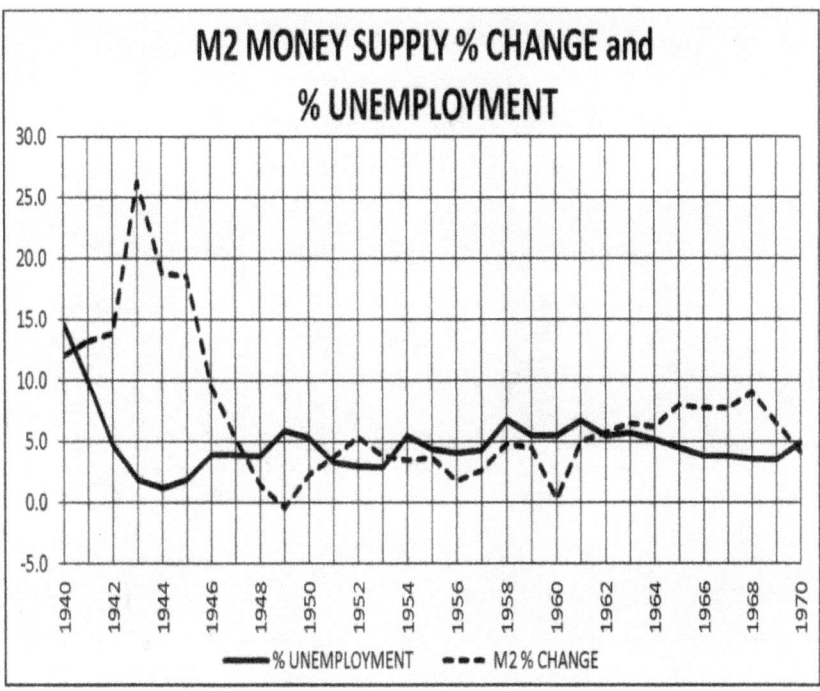

Figure 11. Percent money supply change versus unemployment. 1940—1970.

Figure 11 clearly shows the effect of wartime spending during the 1940s; and also but not as pronounced the increase in spending during the Korean conflict in the 1950s and in Vietnam in the late 1960s.

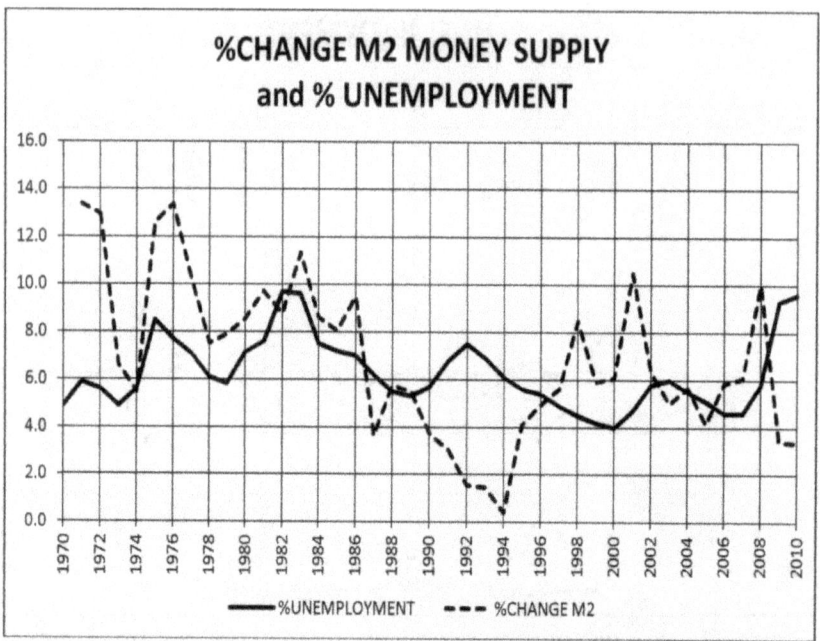

Figure 12. Percent money supply change versus unemployment.
1970—2010.

Figure 12 illustrates a break from the general pattern of the previous charts. There is a spike of increase in money supply and unemployment in the early 1970s. This coincides with the oil embargo which slowed the economy and increased inflation. There is a similar effect in the 1980s when there was high inflation. The interest rates were increased very high by the Federal Reserve at that time. The high interest rates hurt the economy, producing the unemployment. The chart in the 1990s and early 2000s clearly show the recessions of that time.

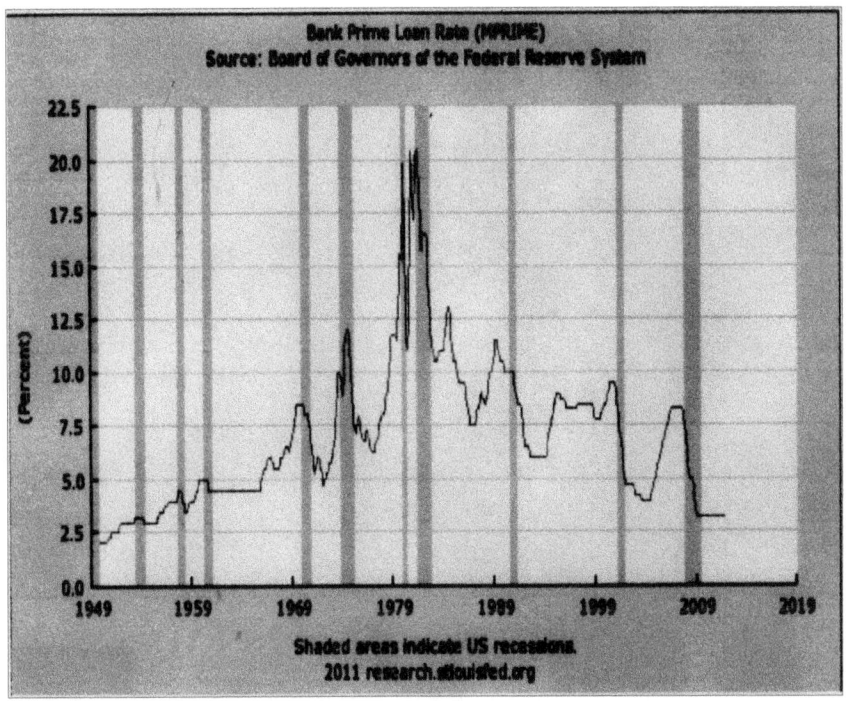

Figure 13. Prime interest rate. 1950—2010.

The data in this chapter shows the correlation between the money supply and panics, depressions and recessions. The next chapter on the creation of money will illustrate the cause of the variations in the money supply; the underlying cause.

Chapter IV
The Creation of Money

From the previous chapter it is clear that depressions and recessions are caused by a reduction of the money supply. To understand how the quantity of money in circulation increases and decreases requires an examination of the operation of the banking system in creating money.

What portion of your money consists of coins and bills? Is not most of your money just an entry in the computer at your bank, rather than bills or coins in your pocket or in your mattress?

To understand how the quantity of money in circulation increases and decreases requires an examination of the operation of the banking system in creating money.

Banks are in the business of creating money by making loans. This is may have started with the goldsmiths storing gold for traders, merchants and whoever had the need for securing their gold. The goldsmith would issue receipts for the gold which he stored. (This may not have been the way modern banking started but it provides a good explanation of how banking operates.)

Because the receipts represented gold; traders and merchants realized that buying and selling using these receipts was easier than using the actual gold. This provided a safer way of conducting business than carrying around gold. The receipts could be traded for goods and services. In this way the receipts for gold in effect became money. Warehouse receipts for other items such as copper or silver have also been used for trading. (Later these receipts would be called banknotes.)

The Creation of Money

The next step in banking was the goldsmith making loans to merchants, traders, and manufacturers. In making these loans the goldsmith could issue gold receipts, banknotes, rather than provide gold.

The goldsmith/banker in making loans charges interest on the loans. This requires that the repayment he receives must exceed the value of the receipts/banknotes that he issued in making the loan. The repayment to the goldsmith/banker must be paid with his own receipts/banknotes, the issued receipts/banknotes of another trusted goldsmith/banker, or in actual gold. The goldsmith banker thus made a profit from making loans.

The next step came from the realization by the goldsmith/banker that he could print receipts for more gold than he actually had in storage. The owners of the gold he had on deposit would never all demand their gold at the same time. So the goldsmith banker could then make loans by printing receipts. In this manner the goldsmith/banker earned profits from effectively creating money. This money was created by the printing of the receipts (later called banknotes).

The goldsmith/banker must necessarily maintain a reserve of gold or gold coins to satisfy the everyday needs of his depositors for gold in the transactions of their business. Like the goldsmith/banker the banks must maintain a reserve to fulfill the routine transactions of their depositors.

Similarly banks today loan money they do not have, by issuing checks or crediting the borrowers account. In this way banks create money.

With the use of credit cards the money is created by the bank paying the bill of the merchant that accepted the credit card and charging the account of the credit card holder. Again the money paid to the seller who accepts the credit card does not come from any account—it is created by the bank at that point in time. The use of a credit card is a loan made by the credit card issuer (bank) to the credit card user. This money is created "out of thin air" since it did not exist until the loan was made.

At the present time the amount of reserves a bank must maintain is set by the Federal Reserve. As an example if the reserve requirement of banks is set at 10%, this means that with $10 million on deposit a bank could make loans to the extent of $9 million. This amount can be greatly expanded by this $9 million being spent and deposited in another bank account acting as an increase in reserves; thus allowing more loans.

When the "goldsmith/banker" receives in repayment the banknotes (gold receipts) which he issued when he made the loan, these notes are then taken out of circulation. The repayment reduces the money supply by the amount of the loan.

The repayment of loans, even in modern banking removes money from circulation—it effectively destroys/cancels out the money created by the loan! So paying off loans reduces the money supply.

When money is created by making a loan and the borrower defaults on the loan, due to inability to pay or by going into bankruptcy, then the money that is not repaid remains in existence. It is not taken out of the money supply as it is when a loan is repaid.

By making loans the banks increase the amount of money in circulation. This increases the money supply. When loans are paid off the money supply is reduced by the amount of the loan.

Prior to 1933, in the United States gold and silver were used as money. In 1933 President Roosevelt required all individuals, partnerships, associations and corporations to turn in all their gold coins, gold bullion and gold certificates to the Federal Reserve. There were exceptions for mining companies and industrial users. Another exception was made for collections of less than $100.00 value.

Silver coins and silver certificates were used for a number of years; discontinued as the value of silver increased and the value of the silver in the coins exceed the face value of the coins.

In 1971 President Nixon severed the fixed dollar value of gold. Since 1933, gold cannot be dug out the ground and used as money. As a result of these actions by President Roosevelt and President Nixon the money supply is composed only of money which is created by the banks. Effectively since 1933 money can only be created by banks by loaning money!

With only a few exceptions the government does not create money. The creation of money is left to the banks!

Prior to 1933 a gold rush would increase the money supply; at times this rescued the country from a depression or recession. At other times it has probably prevented, or delayed recessions or recessions. This is no longer possible as gold is no longer used as money.

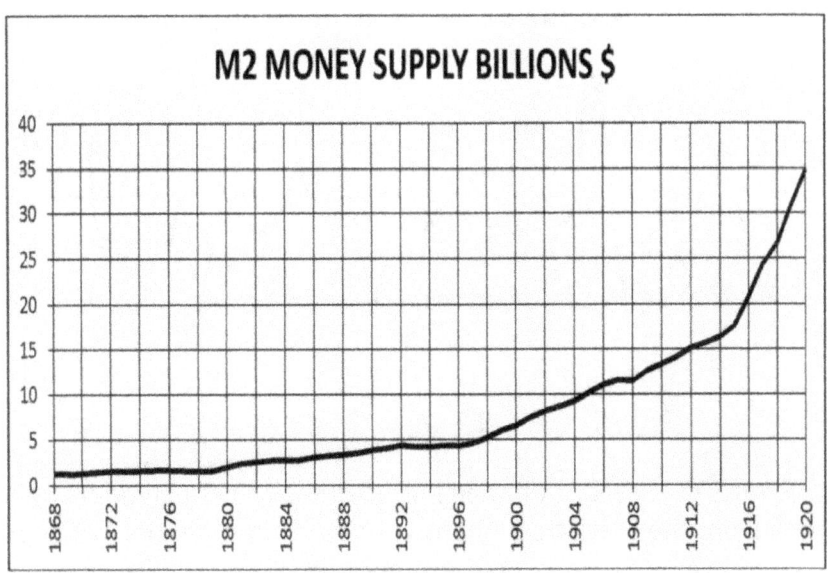

Figure 14. M2 Money supply 1868-1920. From Statistical Abstract of the United States, US Dept of Commerce.

M2 is M1 plus savings and time deposits that is not so readily available for spending. M1 is the money supply that is readily available for spending; currency plus coin plus deposits in banking accounts, etc.

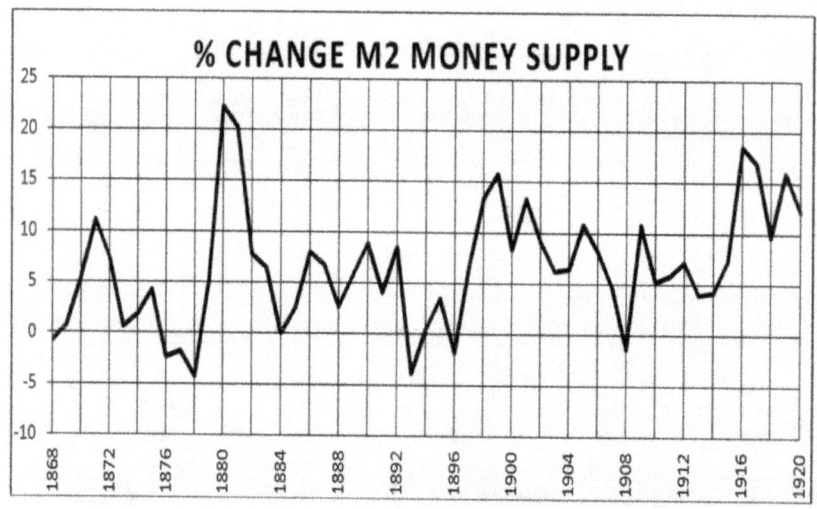

Figure 15. Percent Change M2. 1868--1920. Derived from data from the Statistical Abstract of the United States, US Dept of Commerce.

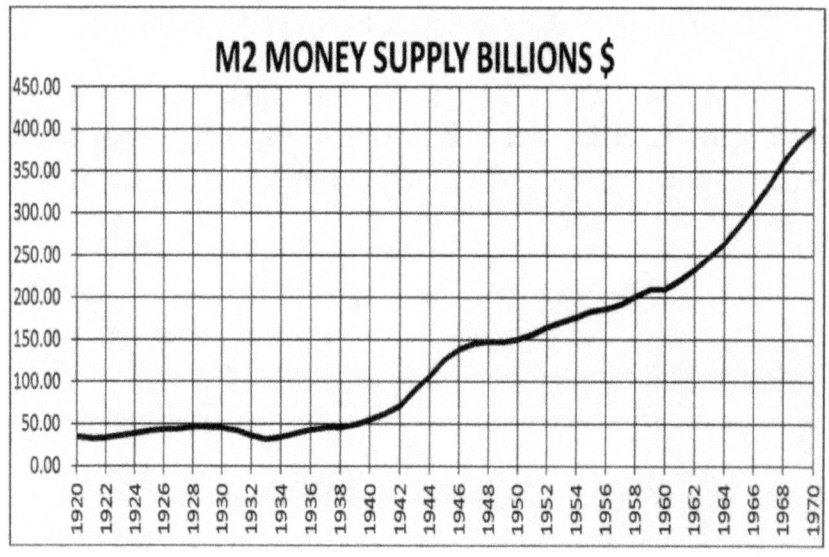

Figure 16. M2 Money supply. 1920--1970. From Statistical Abstract of the United States, US Dept of Commerce.

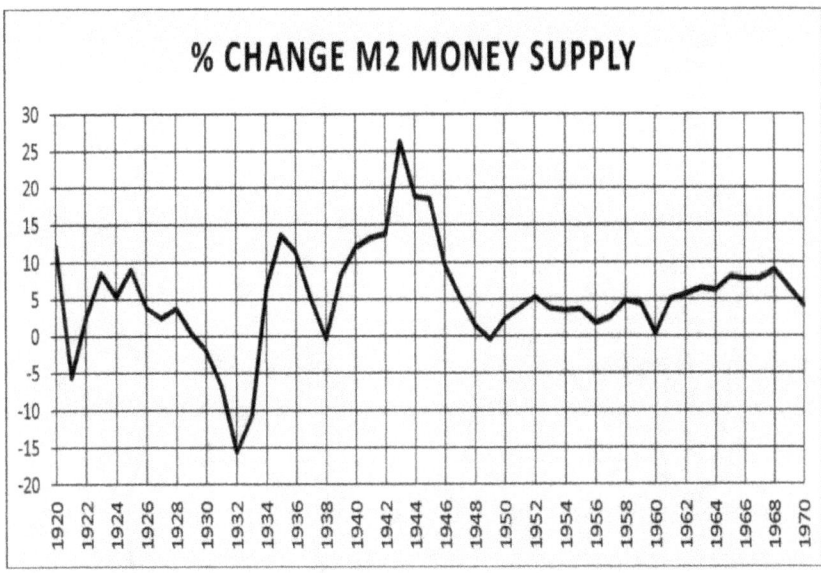

Figure 17. Percent Change M2. 1920—1970. Derived from data from the Statistical Abstract of the United States, US Dept of Commerce.

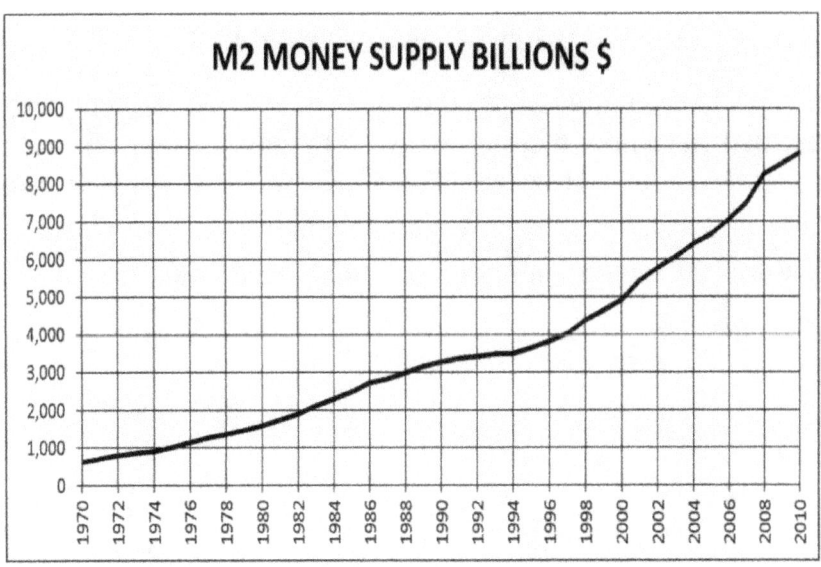

Figure 18. M2 1970—2010. From Federal Reserve Data, St. Louis Federal Reserve Bank.

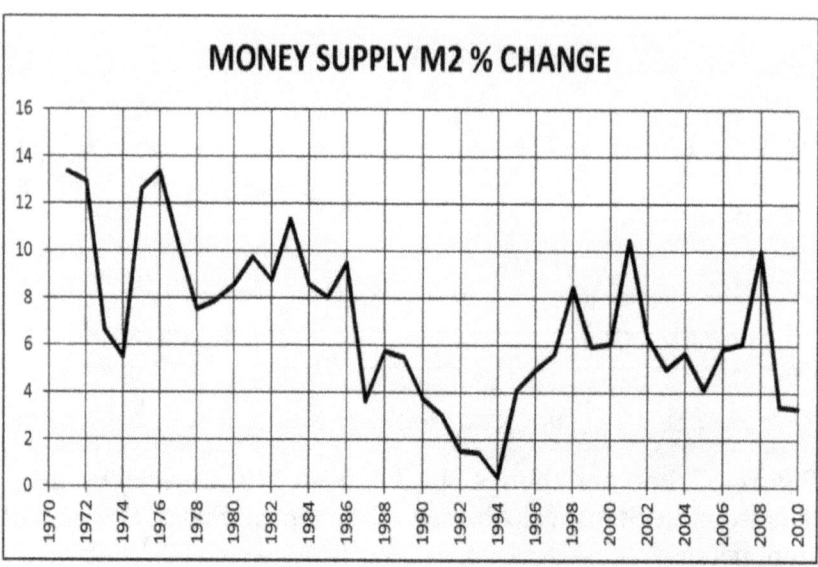

Figure 19. Percent Change M2 1970—2010. Derived from Federal Reserve Data, St. Louis Federal Reserve Bank.

This chapter has shown that money is now only created by banks making loans. The government does not create money. Also shown is how money is created and increases the money supply, and how money is destroyed and reduces the money supply when loans are paid off.

Chapter V
The Cause of Depressions and Recessions.

The cause of depressions and recessions is that when money is created by the banks that debt is created. The previous chapter explained how money is created and destroyed. In creating money more debt is created than money. Money is created by the amount of the loan. **Debt is created to the amount of the loan plus the interest.**

As money is created by borrowing from banks the money supply increases. As loans are repaid the money supply is reduced.

The creation of money is left entirely to the banks! The bank creates money out of nothing when making a loan. The borrower must then pay back the loan amount plus interest. It is done this same way when businesses borrow money. Multiply this by millions of people and thousands of companies borrowing money and this shows the magnitude of the creation of money by banks. If a bank creates a million dollars by loaning it out to a company, an individual or a government (such as a state or foreign government) then more than a million dollars is created in debt.

The increase in debt is always greater than the increase in the money supply!

The payment of a loan takes money out of circulation and requires additional money to cover the interest charges!

The problem with this present system of creating money is that more debt is created than money! Money is

created to the amount of the loan. Debt is created by the amount of the loan plus the interest charges! Thus more debt is created than money! Payment of the loan reduces the money supply!

So for this to work there must be an increase in the money supply year after year. With this increase of the money supply there is a corresponding increase in debt. Yet at some point consumers, farmers, businesses and governments are unable or unwilling to take on more debt. At that time a recession, panic or depression follows due to a reduction in the rate of creation of money. *Thus a recession or depression is a debt crisis!*

The economy can function for some years by creating more money each year; enough money can be created in following years to increase the money supply and pay the interest of the previous years. But this further increases the indebtedness of the individuals, companies, consumers and governments that borrowed. (Money is only created when people, companies or governments borrow money.)

After some years of the creation of money by borrowing the debt will greatly exceed the money supply! Since the indebtedness of companies, consumers, and governments (particularly state and local governments) gradually increases over the years there comes a point where they must reduce their borrowing.

When individuals, companies, and governments reduce their borrowing and continue to make payments on their debt a downward spiral is created which feeds on itself. The reduction of borrowing reduces the rate of creation of money; while the paying of loans takes money out of the money supply. Thus the money supply is reduced or the rate of increase of the money supply is slowed.

Reduction of borrowing by companies and governments typically means reduction of the workforce and reduced buying of supplies. For consumers it usually means putting off some purchases; such as new furniture, new appliances, a new car or remodeling the house or etc. Thus there is a slowdown in buying by consumers.

Reduction of spending by consumers reduces the sales of companies. Companies reduce their spending by reducing their workforce, and reducing their inventory; which means less buying from suppliers. This leads to unemployment which then in turn further reduces sales; this further increases unemployment.

This reduction of business and employment leads to a reduction of tax income for governments at all levels; local, state and federal. At the same time government expenses increase for unemployment and social services. Reduction of the government workforce due to reduced tax income leads to more unemployment. This speeds the downward spiral.

The key item that causes this is the increase in indebtedness that is part of the process of creating money! So this is the cause of recessions and depressions.

In past centuries gold and silver were used as money. A recovery from a "panic", recession or depression could then come about by companies, people and banks going bankrupt or by money, gold or silver, being dug out of the ground to increase the money supply. Gold and silver are no longer money and cannot be dug out of the ground to bring about a recovery.

Only bankruptcies, foreclosures and write off of loans can now reduce the indebtedness of people, individuals and governments. When people and companies go bankrupt the money that was created when they borrowed is not removed from the money supply.

When the amount of debt in relation to the money supply is adequately reduced a recovery can take place!

During a panic banks would fail as depositors withdrew funds to pay debts. A panic would occur when people got the idea that a bank might not have adequate funds to pay all the depositors. During such a time a bank might survive only by demanding borrowers pay their debts immediately; which then could mean withdrawal of funds from other bank accounts; further feeding the crisis.

Bankers at times contributed to the panic, recession or depression by extending too many risky loans. Other bankers may have deliberately made loans that they knew could not be repaid in order to take over farms, ranches or businesses.

Before recovery can take place the amount of debt must be reduced! Recovery from a depression often meant widespread business failures and bankruptcies that reduced the indebtedness of people and companies.

The Klondike gold rush in 1897 and the discovery of gold in Colorado pulled the United States out of the depression that started in 1893; this was comparable in severity with the depression of the 1930s. Gold discoveries in Australia and South Africa helped the world economy recover.

A recovery from a depression or recession can also be created by government spending. Government spending can also prevent a recession or depression. The government spending increases the money supply. This increases the indebtedness of the government. In such a situation the government takes on the excess of debt in relation to the amount of money created. The recovery from the depression of the 1930s came from government spending for arms for WWII. Government borrowing for other wars has had a similar effect.

After a recovery from a depression, panic or recession the cycle starts again. Companies and governments start borrowing again and hiring workers. This borrowing increases the money supply and picks up the economy. Then after some years as the increased borrowing produces more money and even more debt is created until again the indebtedness of individuals, companies and governments becomes too great a burden on the economy and again a panic, depression or recession comes about! Thus over the centuries we have experienced repeated economic cycles, each cycle ending in a panic, recession or depression.

As we saw in Chapter III there is a reduction in the rate of increase in the money supply during recessions and depressions; during the depression of the 1930s there was a shrinking of the money supply. So shrinking of the money supply or the reduction of the usual rate of increase of the money supply is a characteristic of recessions and depressions. This can be shown to be caused, a byproduct, of the way that money is created.

To restate this: The banker making loans increases the money supply. Paying off loans reduces the money supply. Yet there must be some source of money to pay the interest on the loan, typically this is by additional loans made year after year increasing the money supply. These loans that increase the money supply increase the amount of debt more than the increase in the money supply! So after some years the debt becomes excessive.

This method of creating money and putting it into circulation is inherently unstable! When bank depositors or holders of banknotes (gold or silver certificates) demanded

their money, gold or silver, (In the 18th, 19th, and early 20th centuries.) from the bankers this would bring on a business collapse, (panic, recession or depression) because there was never enough gold or silver to cover all the banknotes issued by the banks.

When speculative gambling with money takes place, as with the stock market boom in 1929, and the recent housing bubble, there a great increase in borrowing money. This is a bubble in borrowing from the banks. This also means there is an even bigger and faster increase or bubble in debt.

A bubble or boom becomes restrained by the need for ever more money being put into the bubble to sustain it. Also some of the major players take their money and profits out of the game. The result is that there is not enough money to cover the cost of the debts. No longer is enough money being created to cover the principal plus the interest payments.

This is exactly what happened in the late 1920's that lead to the stock market crash in 1929. Again this occurred recently with the housing bubble!

The only restriction put on the banks creating money is the reserve requirement and the willingness and ability of businesses, farmers and consumers to borrow. Trying to get the economy to recover from a recession has been characterized as "pushing on a string", for even though there is money available for borrowing there is no demand for borrowing money, because of excessive debt—thus the supply of money needed to increase economic activity is not brought into existence.

In 1933 President Roosevelt required all individuals, and companies to turn in their gold coins, gold bullion and gold certificates to the Federal Reserve Banks. Exceptions were made for mining companies, and companies using gold in their products; and some collector's items.

Effectively since 1933, within the US, the only money by which debt could be repaid was by money created by the banks. No longer could money be dug out of the ground; only banks could create money! The only source of new money since then is debt money—only money created with a debt attached greater than the amount of money created!

This cinched the need to have ever more money created by the banks to cover interest payments. This action also insured that governments would have ever increasing debt; because only the government could take on more debt to rescue the country from a recession or depression. If the government did not do this the great burden of debt by businesses, farmers and individuals would keep a recession going.

No longer could money be dug out of the ground to pull the economy out of a recession or depression. Spending by the government on arms performed this function during World War II. Since then government spending on various items have served the same function—such as welfare, social security, Medicare, arms for several wars and etc.

In 1971 President Nixon cut the connection between the value of the dollar and gold, to stop the export of gold from this country. This has had the effect of disconnecting the currencies of other countries from gold also. Thus other countries also rely on bank created money and have the same problem—that is their money is also created by borrowing; thus having the same debt problems!

The downside of this recovery by government spending is increased debt by the government with increased interest payments. Reduction of the interest paid by the government when borrowing would greatly reduce the indebtedness of the government.

There is at this time no other means of pulling a country out of a recession or depression than by increased spending by the federal government! This illustrates the need for a method of creating and putting money into circulation without creating debt; debt free money!

It does not matter what the rate of interest is, at some point the debt will become too excessive to be supported. The greater the rate of creation of money, and thus debt, the sooner the debt crisis will occur. Similarly the greater the interest charged the sooner the debt crisis will occur. So the combination of a greater rate of borrowing and the higher interest charges that are incurred during a "boom", (Investors in the boom are willing to pay higher interest rates to participate in the boom.) by individuals and companies desiring to take part in the boom, the result is a faster and greater build up of debt. Then the more severe will be the crash!

The government does not create money, with the exception of coins, "greenbacks" during the Civil War, and some US Notes (to the extent of $300 million) since then. If the federal government issued money would it have such a large federal deficit?

Congress authorized the Treasury to issue "greenback" dollars in 1862 and 1863 to help finance the Civil War. This was the creation of "debt free" money; the Treasury created the money instead of having banks create the money and loan it to the government at interest.

Debt Crises

A very import aspect of this method of creating money by the banks is the transfer of wealth that takes place; wealth is transferred from those that must borrow (From people, farmers and businesses) to those that profit from the use or production of money.

Unemployment compensation, Social Security payments, and welfare programs transfer the debt from people to the government. But as the creation of debt by borrowing continues over the years a situation has come about whereby the amount of debt is greater than the supply of money, as it is at this time; 2012. One aspect of this that needs to be understood is that if the Federal government were to pay off its debt this would bring about such a shortage of money that disaster would ensue. Just the action of the government balancing its budget would cause a continuing economic problem for the people of this country. This is so because borrowing by the government is a big source of the creation of money into the economy. The removal of this source of money being introduced into the economy and the increase in taxes required to balance the budget would then certainly cause a continuing recession or depression.

There is perhaps a low interest rate, near zero, that would give a stable debt situation. This is because if a loan is not repaid, perhaps because of bankruptcy, then the money created by that loan is not cancelled out as it would be if the loan were repaid, so that amount of money would remain in the money supply.

There is a definite effect on the economy of the "velocity" (Rate at which money circulates through the economy.) of money, however this does not cancel out the effect of the creation of debt when money is created.

It is clear that recessions and depressions are debt crises! No matter the interest rate charged this method of

creating money while creating debt must eventually produce a recession or depression; a debt crisis.

A high interest rate speeds up the rate of creation of debt as also does a higher rate of borrowing (More borrowing per month or year.). Thus a high rate of borrowing at high interest rates as during a boom brings on a debt crisis, recession quicker and harder. Whereas a low rate of borrowing at low interest rates will make the time between the recessions and depressions longer.

Recessions and depression are caused by the method by which money is created by the banks. This applies worldwide.

Summary:

Money is created exclusively by banks making loans.

Interest is charged on these loans by the banks.

When a loan is made the debt is greater than the amount of the loan by the amount of the interest. Therefore the amount of debt created is greater than the amount of money created.

The result after some time is a recession or depression. This the cause of the repetitive cycles of recessions and depressions.

With the present system only a government can continue to borrow and continue to create the money to pull a country out of a recession or depression!

This dramatically illustrates the need for a mechanism of creating debt free money!

It is suggested to the reader to set up a program using an Excel spreadsheet that projects the money supply and debt over a period of years. Set it up with the creation of money (borrowing) at some yearly rate; the interest set at some rate; a repayment rate; then the consequent amount of debt created; run this program for a period of some years.

The following effects should be included: repayments reduce the money supply and the debt; loans increase the money supply; the interest rate plus the loan determines the amount of debt created. Run the program several times varying the interest rate, the repayment rate, the rate of borrowing for a period of years. You will then see that regardless of the variation of these items (interest rate, borrowing rate, and repayment at some point the amount of debt will exceed the money supply!) Also it will show that the higher the interest rate the sooner the debt will exceed the money supply, similarly you will see that the higher the rate of money creation each year the sooner the debt will exceed the money supply. See Chapter IX to set this up.

Chapter VI
The Federal Government and The Federal Reserve

As mentioned in Chapter I panics, depressions and recessions have occurred many times during since the establishment of the United States. In fact they occurred many times prior to the existence of the United States.

During the Revolutionary War, waged to become independent from England, the Continental Congress issued paper money in 1775, called Continentals to pay for the war. The value of these notes dropped to the point that when something had very little value, it "was not worth a continental".

The Bank of the United States was established February 25, 1791. It was a private bank with a portion of the stock funded by the US Government. It handled government funds and tax income. Its charter expired in 1811.

The Second Bank of the United States was chartered in 1817 for 20 years its charter to expire in January 1836. Again it was a private bank with the US Treasury owning a portion of the stock. It was the depository for US government funds. This bank fueled a boom in land prices. It became overextended which created a boom and bust. President Jackson vetoed the extension of its charter in 1834. Jackson then had the US Treasury withdraw the government funds and deposit the funds in state chartered banks.

After the closing of the 2nd Bank of the United States there was an era of "free banking" until the creation of the national banking system in 1863. During this era there were many different private banks issuing banknotes. There were also many bank failures and a number of "panics".

The Federal Government and The Federal Reserve

Congress has assigned its constitutional right to coin money to the banks through the creation of the National Bank system in 1863 and by the creation of the Federal Reserve Banking System in 1913. The right of congress to assign the creation of money to the banks was affirmed by the Supreme Court in the 19th century.

Congress authorized the issuance of greenback dollars in 1862 and 1863 during the civil war to help fund the war. This was during Lincoln's presidency.

In 1863 the National bank system was instituted. This was done to provide a standard currency. This system remained until the establishment of the Federal System in 1913.

The Federal Reserve System was instituted by Congress in 1913. This was done in response to the outrage at the "Money Trust". In 1907 there was a banking panic that threatened the failure of some major banks. J.P. Morgan (Considered the major banker of the "Money Trust".) got some bankers together to solve the problems of the banks.

The Federal Reserve System was set up to be controlled by a board the majority of which were appointed. The Board of Governors of the Federal Reserve System is made up of seven members nominated by the President and approved by the Senate. This met the requirement of President Wilson who was adamant that the system would be publicly controlled; not privately controlled by the bankers. (This public control has been subverted by the appointment to the Board of Governors of bankers or financial industry representatives.)

Banks were required to join the Federal Reserve System and to buy "stock" in the system. This "stock" conveys no property rights nor voting rights as stock in companies normally does. The banks were initially required to do this to provide the initial funding of the system. The banks are paid interest on this stock. Profits of the Federal Reserve System are paid back to the Treasury.

The Federal Reserve Bank acts as a source of reserves for banks; providing emergency loans to banks as needed, and acts as a clearing house (clearing checks and funds between banks). The Board of Governors sets the reserve requirements of the member banks; it also sets the prime interest rate for banks. It also to some extent controls the money supply by buying and selling government securities; to increase the money supply it buys government securities—thus putting more money in circulation; to reduce the money supply it sells government securities—thus taking money out of circulation.

The Federal Reserve System has consistently acted in favor of the banks; fighting inflation by restricting the money supply or raising interest rates to usurious levels. In doing this has put businesses and farmers out of business—as in the 1980s.

The Federal Reserve System has not prevented panics, depressions or recessions as it has not addressed the cause of recessions and depressions. There were several bank panics in the 1930s. President Roosevelt ordered a bank holiday to give the banks a chance to recover.

Since mid 1933 gold has not been used as money in the United States. In 1933 in the United States people were required to turn in their gold money. President Roosevelt had individuals, partnerships and companies turn in to the Federal Reserve Banks all gold coins, gold bullion and gold certificates. Exceptions were made for mining companies and companies using gold in their production of goods. An exception was made for collections less than $100.00 in value.

Spending by the government for armaments for World War II brought about a recovery from the depression of the 1930s. At that time the money supply was increased by borrowing by the government.

In 1971 President Nixon completely cut the connection between gold and money. This was done to prevent the outflow of gold from the United States to other countries. This has had the added effect that money, as gold, cannot be dug out of the ground to pull a country out of a depression or recession.

In the 1980s the Federal Reserve Banks, under Paul Volker, raised the interest rates very high, at one point over 20%. This was done to fight inflation which had been persistently high. The reduction of inflation could have been done by other measures since it was the excessive creation of money by the banks that greatly contributed to this inflation. These high interest rates had a very detrimental economic effect on this country. It increased the value of the dollar in relation to the money of other countries, which has made exports from this country more expensive and made imports cheaper.

This increase in the interest rates in the 1980s increased the rate of increase of debt by businesses and the federal and local governments. It made it more expensive for people, companies and governments to borrow money for projects and for employing people.

In present day practice the banknotes are not printed by the banks, as they were in the past; money is created by crediting the borrowers account in the bank with the amount of the loan, or by issuing a check, wherein the amount of this check is not taken from any account but is charged against the loan and backed only by the loan papers.

Debt Crises

At the present time currency, banknotes, are printed by the Treasury department and sold to the Federal Reserve at the cost of printing which in turn sells them to the banks as needed and demanded by the public. Coins are minted by the Treasury Department and sold to the banks at face value.

The value of money is based on the agreement that it is money and is designated as legal tender backed by the value of securities issued by the US Treasury.

With the advent of social security, welfare programs, and unemployment compensation the effect of a recession or depression has been reduced. This is government spending which in turn usually means an increase in government borrowing. By government borrowing the money supply is increased to pick up the economy; which also means the debt of the government is increased by an amount greater than the increase in the money supply.

The problem with austerity programs is that they are fundamentally flawed. The flaw is this; the repayment of debt reduces the money supply. When a country goes on an austerity program and pays down debt the money supply in that country is reduced. This will turn down the economy in that country due to the reduction of the money supply.

In the United Sates we have the present condition that the debt of the government exceeds the money supply, this is probably true for many governments worldwide.

At the end of April 2012 the US public debt exceeded $15 trillion,(Ref: US Treasury Dept.) and the money supply M2 was $9.8 trillion. (M2 is M1 plus money that is not so readily available, such as certificates of deposits and etc; M1 is the money supply that is readily available for spending—checking accounts, currency, travelers checks and etc..)

The Federal Government and The Federal Reserve

The overall result with the present system of creating money is that to keep their economies operating governments must become ever more in debt. It is impossible to keep economies going without creating ever more debt to supply the money to keep operating. Companies and individuals cannot keep taking on ever more debt to supply the operating money needed. Only governments can and have done this!

The banking/financial business, and primarily through the action of the Federal Reserve Bank, controls the economy by the control of the money supply. This is done worldwide by the central banks of countries. While the banks create the money they increase debt at a greater rate than the rate at which they create money. Thus the creation of depressions and recessions is directly due to the action of banks!

This is not just a problem for the US, similar cycles of panics, recessions and depressions have happened worldwide in many nations. It is the curse of the method by which money is created and put in circulation by many nations. The recent housing bubble was a housing bubble in many nations around the world! The resulting economic downturn is also a worldwide problem.

There is a reduction in the rate of increase in the money supply during recessions and depressions. Shrinking of the money supply or the reduction of the usual rate of increase of the money supply is a characteristic of recessions and depressions.

The above illustrates the need for a method of creating money without creating debt. This was done during the US civil war by the Treasury issuing "greenback" dollars.

Chapter VII
Trade

One of the most important effects on trade is the relative value of the currency of one country in relation to the value of the currency of the trading partner. The effect of the high interest rates imposed in the 1980s by the Federal Reserve under Paul Volker was to push the value of the American dollar high in relation to other countries. This has negatively impacted the ability of American companies to sell their products to other countries and to compete with imports.

Since about 1970 another factor has entered; so called free trade. Why has free trade been instituted? Consider a bank that loans money to another country; say Citibank in the 1970s loaning a 100 million dollars to Mexico. To pay back this money in American dollars Mexico must collect by trade one hundred million dollars plus the dollars required to cover the interest charges. (At one point the US Government stepped in to rescue Mexico and thus allow the banks to be repaid.) Mexico can only do this by trading goods and services worth more than the amount of the loan. If the trade with Mexico is balanced, that is the value of goods exported, in dollars, is equal to the value of goods imported, in dollars, then Mexico will not receive the dollars to pay back the loan plus interest. So to pay off this loan to the bank Mexico must then have a imbalance of payments with the US in favor of Mexico.

This works out that if the USA has balanced trade and thus a balance of payments (money out of the country equal to money into the country), the foreign entities, governments or companies that have borrowed money from the US banks will not receive enough US dollars to pay back the balance of their loan plus interest! Thus the banks making loans in US dollars need "free", unbalanced trade, (more money out of this country than money back into this country from other countries) to have their loans repaid with interest. Thus it is of interest to the banks to have more imports than exports for America!

Similar problems occur for other countries engaging in trade, particularly in trading with countries with very low labor costs. Trading with China is a problem for other countries because of China keeping its currency at a low relative value,

Large multinational corporations also benefit from "free" trade by producing goods "offshore" (where "offshore" represents anywhere besides the US) by taking advantage of cheap labor in other countries. Some companies such as GE also have a financial division that engages in loaning money. Thus we have both companies and banks benefiting from "free", unbalanced trade.

"Free" trade has resulted in a large portion of the money created in the US to be exported to other countries without a corresponding return flow. Thus we are exporting money and jobs to other countries. An example is NAFTA; manufacturing jobs have been exported to Mexico and we import goods and export money; which mostly goes to the international companies not to the Mexican employees of these companies.

The most glaring example however is the trade with China. China has been allowed to artificially keep the value of their money low in relation to the US dollar, thus subsidizing exports. Americans have gotten poorer year after year since for about the last 40 years. (See the "Pooring of America" by Dr. Ravi Batra. (5))

Free trade has been imposed on America by both the Democratic Party and the Republican Party. Both of these political parties accept money from the banks and multinational companies to impose their will. (The banks were allowed to merge and become megabanks with correspondingly greater influence on politics; too big to fail) Our politicians of both parties have contributed to this situation. The Republicans say the Democrats are wrong. The Democrats say that the Republicans are misguided. They are both right!

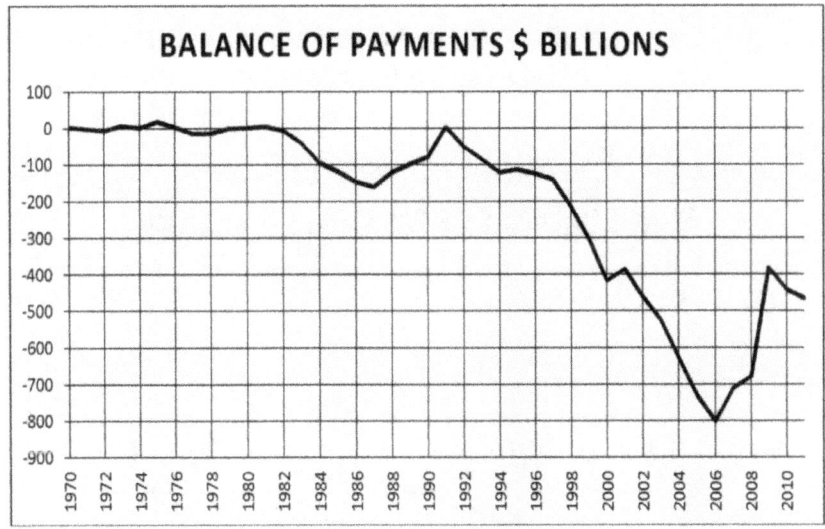

Figure 20. Balance of payments. 1970—2010. From data of the U.S. Census Bureau, Foreign Trade Division.

This figure shows the imbalance of payments of the US. This is the outflow of dollars from the US during this period of time.

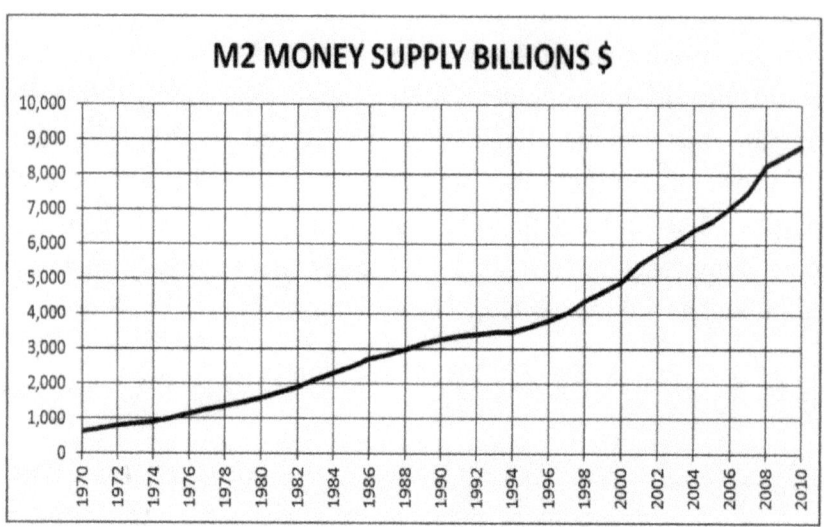

Figure 21. M2 1970—2010. From Federal Reserve Data,
Federal Reserve Bank, St. Louis

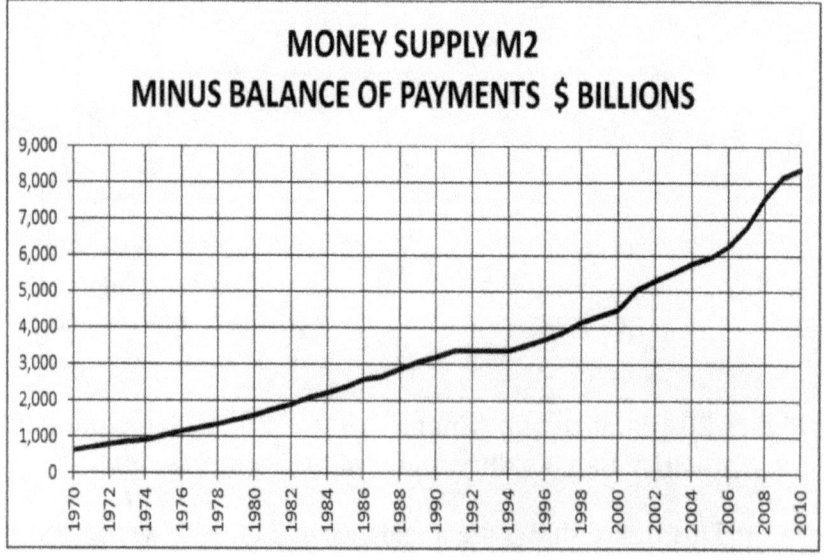

Figure 22. M2 money supply minus Trade deficit, Billions
1970—2010.

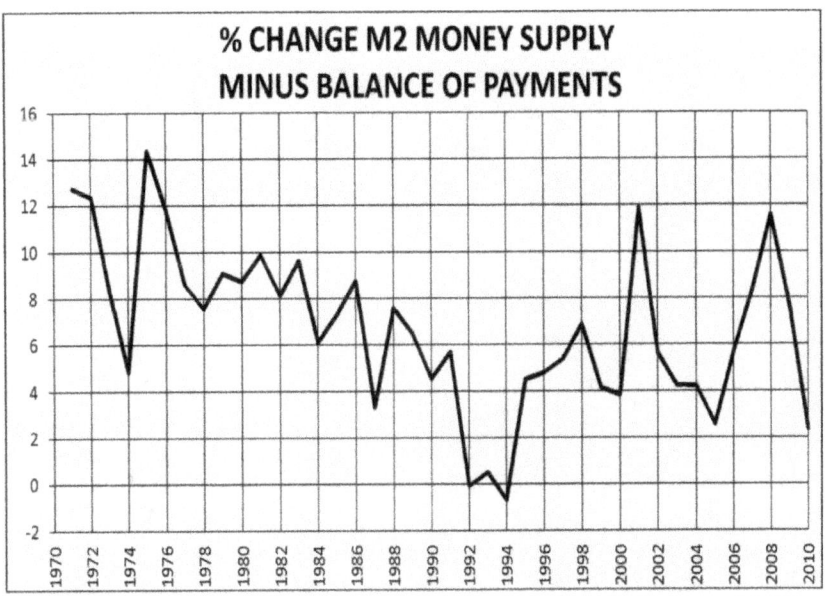

Figure 23. M2 money supply minus Trade deficit % Change 1970—
2010.

Chapter VIII
Solutions/Corrective Actions

The first thing that must be done to solve this problem is to understand that the present system of creating money and putting it into circulation is the cause of depressions and recessions. This system/method of creating money creates more debt than money—in ever increasing amounts! It is important to understand that recessions and depressions are indeed debt crises!

There are a number of alternatives for the US: (Similar actions for other countries also must be done.)

1. Continue on the present path of austerity, this means a continuing recession. Cutting the budget and/or balancing the budget will push the economy further downward into a depression.

2. Government spending increase to help the economy. With the present system of money creation this means increasing the federal debt.

3. Have the government issue United States Notes as was done in the civil war while Lincoln was president. Use these funds for projects to stimulate the economy; renewing infrastructure, rescuing state governments and etc. This would not increase the debt!

4. Enact laws to limit interest rates to less than 5%; particularly on consumer loans such as credit cards, doing this immediately would do much to help restore the economy!

5. Other ways? Have banks write off and or partially write off loans?

Does it make good sense for the Federal government to have banks create money and borrow this money from the banks at interest?

The present debt crisis is a great problem and continuation of the present system of creating money means continuation of recessions and depressions; debt crises! This also means continuation of the present recession and consequent poverty and joblessness for many worldwide! Even if some solution is worked out for the present debt crisis if the system is not changed another recession will occur in a number of years!

So though this is a time of a great problem it is also the time when great solutions can be created! Perhaps by the US government creating projects to renew the infrastructure of the US by having the Treasury issue "greenback dollars", or issue funds to the states for this renewal. This could also be done in the Eurozone and worldwide. Perhaps projects such as bringing water to deserts should be done; think big not small, this not a time for bewailing problems but to take action.

Perhaps it would be possible for congress could select some projects; say highway construction and repair and have the Treasury issue the funds to the transportation department for this. Or issue grants funded by the treasury to rescue state governments as a way to get the country out of the present recession/depression.

Let us make the year 2012 be a year of renewal and a better future.

Another partial and temporary solution for the present economic worldwide problem would be for the Central Banks, such as the European Central Bank, and the Federal Reserve Bank in the US to buy up much of the debt of the governments from the governments. In the US this would work out as the Federal Reserve buying much of the debt of the US Government and of the various state governments. This would be in effect the Central Banks bailing out the various governments. This would remove the world wide "debt crisis" that is a product of the banks creating the money and the "debt" of the debt crisis.

Alternatively the banks must write off, either wholly or partially loans to the governments of many countries! If this is not done the likely result will be political unrest and the rise of political leaders taking over countries while blaming some group for the economic problems or on some ethnic group or immigrants much as Hitler did during the "Great Depression" of the 1930s. This political unrest has already started in Greece and is likely to occur soon in other countries such as Spain. In this country, the United States, there is already a trend in this direction; of blaming immigrants, while the true cause the debt crisis is not being addressed. This can lead to revolutions and possibly wars with the result being even more human suffering and destruction!

Banking and Finance

When the Federal Reserve Banking System was created in 1913 it was conceived as a way to put the banks under public control instead of being controlled by the "Money Trusts". The Board of Governors was and is appointed by the president. This has not worked out because primarily the appointments to the Board of Governors have been bankers or economists from the banking sector. The FOMC (Federal Open Market Committee) also has as its' appointed members bankers or bank friendly economists.

The Federal Reserve System should be made part of the Treasury Department and regulation of banks made more stringent. The Graham-Bliley act should be repealed and the rules separating commercial and investment banking put back in place so that Federal Deposit insurance does not rescue investment banks that have made bad investments or speculation. There is also the need to regulate and limit the operation of domestic banks, particularly commercial banks, in other countries.

Very large banks must be broken up into smaller banks, no bank should be of a size that is "too big to fail", nor should any bank be allowed to become so large that it could dictate terms to the Federal Government. It would be wise to impose a transaction tax on trading of stocks, futures, hedging and etc to inhibit transactions which are just highly speculative.

Very large companies should be broken up; the size of companies should be limited to maintain competition.

A way of creating money and putting money into circulation that does not create more debt than money must be set up. At a minimum enough debt free money must be created so that the gross debt of people, farmers, companies and governments does not keep increasing to the point of a debt crisis; recession or depression.

The Treasury should be issuing money such as the "greenbacks" as were issued during the civil war and not relying on the banks to create our money. If the Treasury issued the money then the national debt would cease to increase. The rate of increase of the money supply should match the needs of the economy. Would this be giving the government a dangerous power? Is this more dangerous than going to the banks and borrowing money to operate on and continuing to increase the federal debt and the continuation of recessions an depressions?

Congress should select many projects; say highway construction and repair and have the Treasury issue the funds, not borrowing the money, to the transportation department for this purpose. Or issue grants to rescue state governments as a way to get the country out of the present recession/depression.

By the treasury issuing the currency the personal income tax could be eliminated. Not all taxes should be eliminated. Tariffs would be desirable for maintaining a balance of trade. Other taxes as on corporations and banks should be used to cover the expenses of regulating them and for the privilege of operating in this country and having the protection of our laws.

Alternatively perhaps the Federal Government should issue money in an amount that would be equal to the added debt that is required to cover the interest created by the issuing of money by the banks. This money could be issued to finance such programs as social security, medical care, unemployment compensation and aid to college students, road repair and etc..

Usury laws should be reinstated that limit the rate of interest that can be charged for loans and credit cards to 5% or less.

These solutions should be used in other countries also as many of them have experienced similar problems caused by the same method of creating money and creating more debt!

If inflation is to be fought under the present banking system it should be done by increasing the reserve requirements of the banks and not by raising interest rates. The high interest rates set by Volker seriously damaged the American economy; putting many small companies out of business and many family farmers out of business; (They could no longer afford to borrow for operating expenses or borrow to buy seed for their next crop.); unbalancing trade, thus creating added unemployment.

Coxey(6) has proposed a system of local banks that would be operated as a public service, effectively creating banks that would be "PUBs" (Public Utility Banks, my name for his banking proposal.).

Jesus Huerta De Soto proposes (Money, Bank Credit, and Economic Cycles) that banks be required to have 100% reserves; thus not able to create money but only loan money that they have. This would require another source of money for an increase of economic activity with the increase of the population; the government would be the logical source of this needed increase.

Corporations and Trade

The charters/rules by which companies are granted incorporation must be changed. Corporations are certainly not individuals that have a right to free speech. Corporations should not be allowed to have any political rights lest they gain too great an influence over the government.

The US needs to get out of the WTO (World Trade Organization) and the "Free Trade" treaties and bring jobs back to America or at least invoke the WTO clause allowing tariffs for to maintain a balance of payments—unbalanced trade can make one country poorer in relation to another country. No country can continue to prosper which depends on others to produce a large part of its goods and services. Presently free trade is a race to the bottom with the lowest priced labor getting the work; tending for the work to go to places that violate the human rights of the workers.

The WTO has rules which prohibit the taxing of certain financial transactions, such as stock market trading. This is another reason to get out of the WTO (Also the WTO has set restrictions on the use of vitamins and food supplements, which have not yet been implemented in the US.).

Constitutional Change

The constitution needs to be amended in two regards:

Companies should not be recognized as people and should not have the rights of people but only have rights given to them explicitly by their charter.

Treaties will other countries should not override the laws of the US!

Wars.

We also must get out of foreign wars, as quickly as possible. They have become outrageously expensive, not just in terms of money but also in the lives of our armed forces but also in the lives of the people where we are fighting—we must find a better way! Under the present way of creating money the cost of war rushes us toward a new debt crisis—recession or depression!

By far the most important item is to increase the awareness people in regard as to what is being done by their government and demand change.

Chapter IX
Money Supply/Debt Projection

This is a method of demonstrating on your computer the problem with the present method of creating money by projecting debt and money supply over a period of years. This is applicable to this country, the USA, and also other countries.

This is based on the principles in the Chapter IV, The Creation of Money:

1. Money is created by the banks making loans.

2. The interest charges on the loans creates more debt than money.

3. Payments on the loans reduce the money supply as these payments take money out of circulation.

So the program is set up to increase the money supply year after year by loans being made. As seen in the graphs of money supply in the previous chapters this is the usual situation. The increase in money supply only comes about by individuals, companies and government borrowing.

Then the debt is projected; loan plus interest minus payments; next the money supply is projected, new money created by borrowing minus payments on the loan.

Using Excel 2007 spread sheet.

NAMEs are assigned and used in the formulas. And then values are assigned to each NAME.

Money Supply/Debt Projection

To assign Names Select "Formulas" then "Name Manager" then "New" and enter the Name you want to use and enter the value it refers to such as =0.05 for indicating 5%.

By assigning Names to the items used in the formulas you can, by changing the value of the Names get the results with the new values.

The rate of borrowing is set at some rate of increase of the money supply of the previous year; in the program this is named LOANRATE.

LOANRATE =1.05 sets rate of increase of new money 5%

The interest is named INTRATE and is set at for example 0.05 for 5%.

INTRATE =0.05 sets the interest rate at 5%; rate charged on new money created.

The amount of the payments is named as PAY and is set at a percentage of the debt, for example setting PAY=0.05, would set the payments at 5% of the debt.

PAY =0.08 sets repayment rate at 8%; 8% of loan paid each year

If you graph DEBT and MNYSUP (money supply) for a period of years you will see the changes in the graph immediately when you change the value of LOANRATE, INTRATE or PAY. Try running with different values of each of the above.

Example assigns row 8 to years; A8 "YEAR" then sequential year numbers 1 to 25 in B8 through Z8 for example for 25 year projection

In A9 enter "MNY VOLUME"   Row 9 then shows volume of money in for each year. Previous money supply times Loan rate.

In A10 enter "LOAN INC"   Row 10 then shows the incremental increase in the loan. Money volume (MNY VOLUME, Row 9) minus previous money supply (MONEY SUP, Row 15). The increase in the money volume is by the increase of the loan (LOAN INC, Row 10) that year.

In A11 enter "TOT LOAN"   Row 11 then shows the total of the loan; Loan increment (LOAN INC, row 10) plus previous total loan (TOT LOAN).

In A12 enter "PAYMENTS"   Row 12 then shows amount of payment.   Total loan (TOT LOAN, Row 11) times payment rate (PAY).

In A13 enter "INTEREST"   Row 13 then shows the interest charge. Interest rate (INTRATE) times total loan (TOT LOAN, Row 11).

In A14 enter "DEBT"   Row 14 shows amount of total debt. Total loan (TOT LOAN, Row 11) plus interest (INTEREST, Row 13) minus payment (PAYMENTS, Row 12).

In A15 enter "MONEY SUP"   Row 15 shows money supply. Money volume (MNY VOLUME, Row 9) minus payment (PAYMENTS, Row 12).

Example set up:

In B8 and remainder of row 8 for number of years to run enter the year numbers, say 1 through 25.

Money Supply/Debt Projection

In B9 and B15 enter the starting value of money you want to use, set to 10,000,000 in example runs.

No entry in B10 through B14.

In C9 enter "=B15*LOANRATE", Then copy this and paste it in D9 and the rest of row 9 for the number of years (25 years in example) you want to run the program.

In C10 enter "=C9-B15". Copy and paste in row 10 as above.

In C11 enter "=C10+B14". Copy and paste in row 11 as above.

In C12 enter "=C11*PAY". Copy and paste in row 12 as above.

In C13 enter "=C11*INTRATE". Copy and paste in row 13 as above.

In C14 enter "=C11+C13-C12". Copy and paste in row 14 as above.

In C15 enter "=C9-C12". Copy and paste in row 15 as above.

This will show the items listed for the number of years you have projected. By changing the values of the NAMES you can change each item and show the results of that change.

You can in addition make charts of the results—for example putting debt and money supply on a line chart, as shown below.

You can also add to this showing the change or percent change in another row.

Using the basic principles more complex projections could be run This projection is valid for the country as a whole; showing the total debt and the money supply, though actual situation is different because of varying interest rates and amount of money borrowed by governments, companies and individuals. More complex projections could be performed by running on a monthly basis and changing the interest rate, payment rate and etc on a monthly basis. .

Charted results:

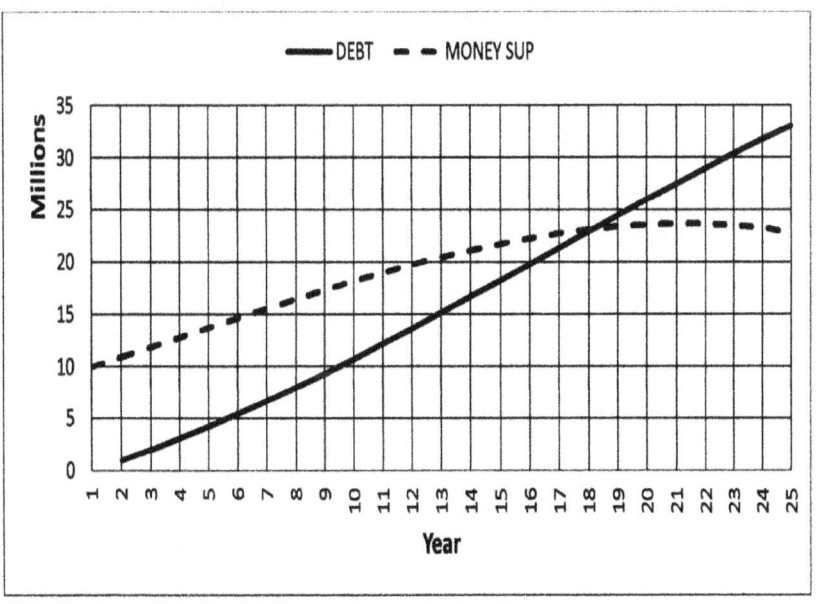

Figure 24. Money Supply/Debt Projection I.

This chart, figure 24, is based on the formulas as stated with the increase by loans set at 10% of the Money supply. The interest rate was set at 5% of the debt; the payment rate at 8% of the debt. The starting amount in B9 and B15 was set at $10,000,000.

The money supply decreases after the debt becomes greater than the money supply because the payments are set at a percentage of the debt. The payments become so large that the money supply is being reduced by the large payments.

Money Supply/Debt Projection

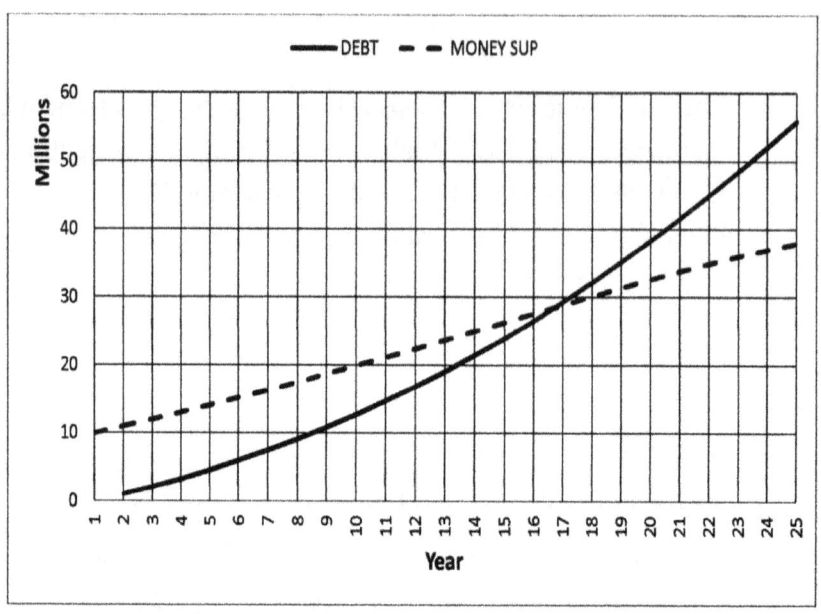

Figure 25. Money Supply/Debt Projection II.

Payment rate reduced to 5%; loan rate increase same at 10% of money supply; interest rate at 5%.

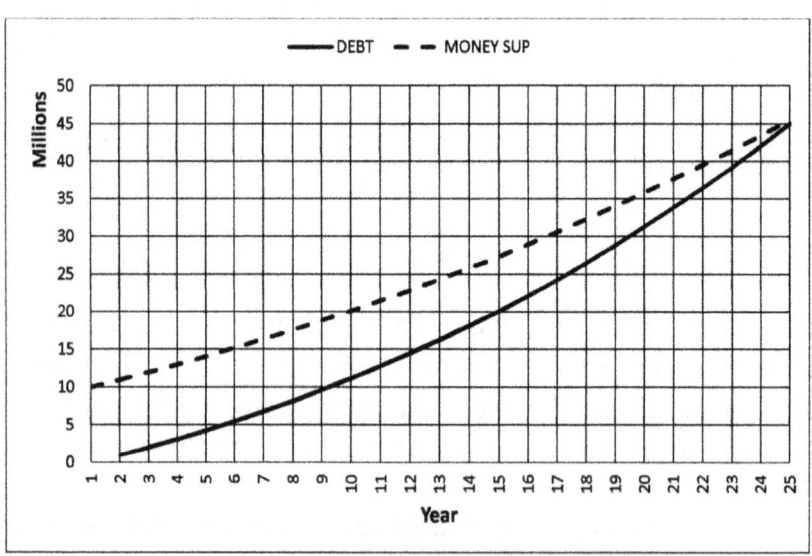

Figure 26. Money Supply/Debt Projection III.

Interest rate reduced to 2%: loan rate increase same at 10% of money supply; payment same at 5%.

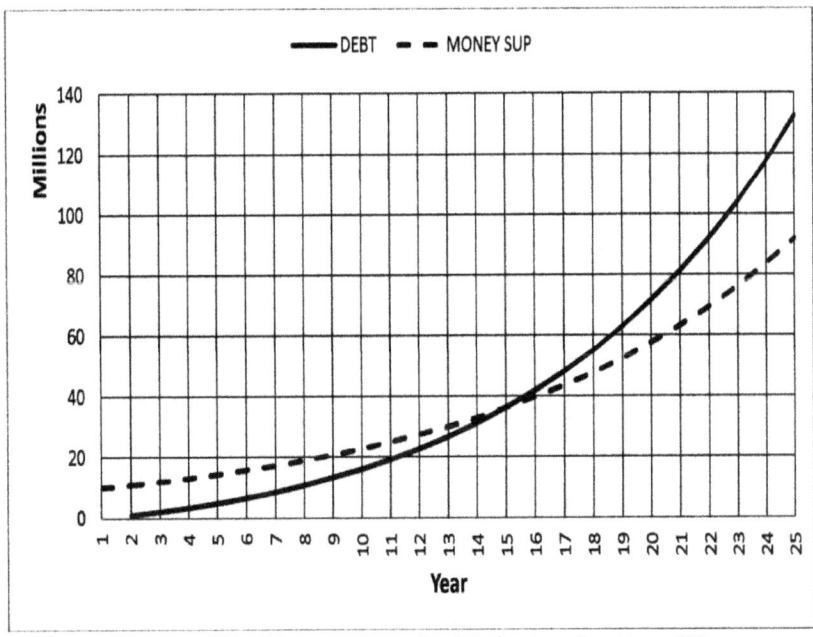

Figure 27. Money Supply/Debt Projection IV.

Formula changed such that increase in loan increases 10% of money volume each year instead of 10% of money supply as in previous charts;   Interest rate at 5% repayment at 5%.   This makes the money supply and debt rise much faster.

References:

1. "Panics" are so called because prior to Deposit insurance when there was the threat of imminent bank failure people would rush to get there money out of the bank before it closed down from lack of money—there was an actual panic of people rushing to get their money.

2. Kondratief cycle: This is a theory by Kondratiev; a theory of major economic cycles.

3. Buying on margin is the practice of buying stock by paying only a small portion of the cost, say 10%, effectively borrowing from the remainder of the price from the stock broker, with the idea that one would make money then by selling at a higher price than the purchase price.

4. "A Primer on Money", Subcommittee on Domestic Finance, Committee on Banking and Currency, House of Representatives, 88th Congress, 2d Session, August 5, 1964, Wright Patman

5. "The Pooring of America", Dr. Ravi Batra

6. "The Coxey Plan", Jacob Selcher Coxey

Bibliography:

1. "Secrets of the Temple, How the Federal Reserve Runs the Country", William Greider.
2. "Debt Virus", Jacques S. Jaikaran, M.D.
3. "Money, Bank Credit, and Economic Cycles", Jesus Huerta De Soto.
4. "The Story of Money", Norman Angell
5. "The Economic Problem", Robert L. Heilbroner
6. "Money Supply", Anna J. Schwartz
7. "World Rollover", C. V. Myers
8. "Encyclopedia of Economics", Douglas Greenwald
9. FRED, Federal Reserve Bank, St Louis
10. National Bureau of Economic Research
11. 117th Statistical Abstract of the United States, 1977, The National Data Book, US Department of Commerce, Economics, and Statistics Administration, Bureau of the Census.
12. "Historical Beginnings…The Federal Reserve", Roger T. Johnson (Federal Reserve Bank of Boston)

About the Author

Victor W. Hatch
Engineer, Inventor, Musician.
Born February 25, 1931 on a farm in
northwestern Oklahoma.

www.ingramcontent.com/pod-product-compliance
Lightning Source LLC
Chambersburg PA
CBHW051220170526
45166CB00005B/1977